Creating a Luxury Garden

Creating a Luxury Garden

H. G. Witham Fogg

The Garden Book Club
121 Charing Cross Road
London WC2 H0EB

First published in Great Britain 1975 by
John Bartholomew and Son Ltd

This special Garden Book Club edition
first published 1976

ISBN 0 70281 052 5

Printed in Great Britain

CONTENTS

CHAPTER 1

HOUSE AND GARDEN

A GARDEN should be regarded as a continuation of the house and not, as so often is the case, something quite apart. This is made easier by the creation or extension of terraces and patios where plants are grown. These create the illusion of continuity between house and garden and the effect is even more convincing when walls and fences are covered with climbers and other wall plants.

The planning and making of gardens is a subject that has interested men and women for centuries and there is something very satisfying in seeing a carefully thought out design becoming a reality. Gardening should not be regarded as a necessary chore but as a satisfying activity. The garden should be a haven of rest and peace; a place where it is possible to get away from the pressures of life and relax.

The introduction of ornamental walls, decorative hedges, window-boxes, and sink gardens give added interest, while properly made paths, drives, screens and home extensions are all assets. Where there is space, a garden pool or even a swimming-pool could be installed. If provision can be made for the erection of a summer-house, a sauna and a barbecue area as well as a children's corner, one can indeed have a pleasure garden for family and friends to enjoy.

We can include in our plans the growing of vegetables and fruit which since they can be used within hours of being gathered, possess that fine fresh flavour so often lacking in supplies bought in shops. Unusual vegetables which are not generally available in the markets can be grown also. We shall not then have to depend on the tired-looking vegetables and indifferent fruit displayed at the green-grocers.

TOOLS FOR THE JOB

A good and even indifferent gardener needs the right tools. It is always worth buying high quality stainless steel forks and spades. These are strong, light, easy to use, and with care, will last a life-time. Flat forks are useful on heavy soil. Tools made of iron or steel need cleaning after use, and washing them or rubbing the metal parts with an oily rag before putting them away will keep them in fine condition. Machines and electrically powered tools are becoming popular but nevertheless, there are various standard tools which every gardener needs.

Apart from forks, spades, rakes and hoes, including the Dutch hoe, hand forks, trowels, shears, secateurs, syringe, water cans and a wheelbarrow, should be regarded as essentials.

There are many firms making reliable gardening implements and for over fifty years, 'Wolf Brand' tools have been widely used in many parts of the world. It is claimed that there is a Wolf tool for every garden operation. One unique feature is the handle, which can be fitted to any Wolf tool by means of a simple tap on the ground. There is no need for nails or screws for the handle stays tight and if necessary can be removed by a simple twist.

CHAPTER 2

SCREENS AND WALLS

ALTHOUGH MANY gardens may not be large enough to allow for the inclusion of architectural features most gardens can be vastly improved by the addition of trellis screens, fences, pergolas and archways as well as by sundials and bird baths. These additions give distinction and make the garden more pleasing for the greater part of the year.

Trellis work can be used to form a screen between two sections of the garden. Well built and clothed with attractive plants, it helps to lift the garden out of the common-place. Such screens need to be built rigidly, for high wind pressure can ruin a weak construction. One has often seen dilapidated trellis work, caused by weak supporting posts. The posts should be of stout timber, preferably 4in. × 3in. The height of the trellis will depend on individual needs but the base of the posts should be buried at least 18in. If the buried part is first painted with a good preservative or dipped in creosote it will be kept from rotting. Creosote, however, can have an adverse effect on plants fixed to the trellis.

If the posts are set in concrete so much the better. While the concrete is hardening, the posts must be secured by temporary stays. An alternative is to bury concrete posts which reach just above ground level and bolt the wooden posts to them. This prevents the wood coming into contact with soil and so lengthens the life of the posts.

Trellis can be made in various designs such as squares, diamonds, rectangles and other geometrical shapes. The wood used must be strong enough to support the growth of roses and climbing plants. Near the house, on a patio or on a courtyard wall, the wood used can be planed and painted white instead of the more usual staining.

SCREEN WALLS

Using a screen wall is a sensible way of dividing up space without sacrificing continuity, an important point nowadays when space is at a premium. At the same time, the screen will bring seclusion to the patio and other parts of the garden and also provide a decorative pattern of light and shade.

In the last few years the screen wall has become popular in both domestic and public buildings in the form of pierced concrete blocks. These are admirable for the purpose, economical and made by several manufacturers in a variety of patterns. Mostly, the block designs are based on geometric forms, circles, rectangles, squares, stars or crosses. However, as concrete is a plastic material, the possibilities are endless.

For houses, the concrete screen wall has been used successfully in this country in various ways. Internally, it may be used as a room-divider, or as a screen in halls and entrances. It has also been used to good effect for garage walls, and of course it is excellent for hiding the coal shed or the dustbins.

In the garden, the screen wall can – if chosen and placed with care – shelter effectively and decoratively the corner of a terrace, an exposed patch of lawn or even a back-yard. It can also be used instead of the conventional fence, or as a background for plants. In general, a well-designed screen wall can add a great deal to the appearance of a garden. However, the use of concrete blocks for screen walls is by no means confined to the house and garden. Plenty of examples exist where infilling panels of these blocks have been used for framed buildings – offices, flats or public buildings – in entrance halls, corridors and circulation spaces. In external walls, glass has, of course, generally been added as a protection from weather, except in parking buildings where pierced blocks provide good ventilation.

These blocks are very easily laid; plinth, pilaster and coping units are usually available for stability and neatness of appearance. In some cases, reinforcement is placed in the jointing mortar or cast into the cavities of pilaster units. Most types of concrete screen wall can be assembled on a 'do-it-yourself' basis.

Blocks are made in different face sizes, depending on design, but are normally 4in thick; units 12in square are common. There is a choice of colour, as blocks can be made with white or coloured cements as well as grey, and sometimes with different coloured aggregates. At present, there are several standard designs made in this country, which may be changed and developed from time to time; the scope for variety and invention is, of course, infinite. Perhaps the simplest of all concrete screen walls, is that built of standard hollow concrete blocks laid with the cavities exposed. These can be extremely effective as well as cheap.

Screen block walls need a good foundation. For this dig out a trench and ram in hardcore to a depth of 6 to 10in according to the height of the wall, the width being 1 to 2ft. Take care not to soil the face of light-coloured screen blocks and make sure that the top of the wall and pillars are so placed that water drains off easily.

It is possible to make your own screen walling blocks and there are firms which supply moulders with mixing and making instructions.

THE ORNAMENTAL WALL

At some time or other most gardeners have had a desire for a wall of some kind in the garden, or have wished away the one that was there! It can be depressing when the dining-room looks straight out on to a wall whether it be one of red brick or something more weather-worn, although perhaps the less common stone wall is not undesirable. Walls do have some advantages for not only do they give privacy, but they provide shelter from cold winds, and often allow the growing of plants which could not otherwise be cultivated.

There are various trained fruit trees which can be accommodated on sheltering walls, while many graceful climbers can be employed both to give colour and hide the bareness. These include the summer and winter flowering jasmines for north and east walls, and ceanothus and wistaria for south or west walls. Honeysuckles, clematis, cotoneaster, climbing roses and pyracanthas will grow against walls whatever the aspect.

When such subjects make most of their new growth several feet from the ground, which is usually what is wanted, a few evergreen flowering plants judiciously placed against the foot of the wall, prevents any bareness near ground level. Even when the walls are away from the house, they will look better clothed with some kind of plant life.

It is not difficult to arrange for light supports to keep the growths in position. Old brick or stone walls can be made most attractive by removing some of the stones, filling the cavities with good soil, and planting flowering subjects usually grown in the rock garden. It is best to keep to plants which can stand a certain amount of drought, such as yellow alyssum, arenaria, aubrietia, alpine pinks, lithospermum, potentillas, dwarf campanulas, saxifrages, sedums and sempervivums.

There is quite another kind of wall which can be made without much trouble, and which can be most useful for increasing the beauty of a garden, as well as hiding unsightly places, or providing a windbreak. This is known as a dry wall, and can be made without the use of mortar. The soil used must be very fine and is best put through a small mesh sieve.

The building procedure is simple, first a layer of soil, then the stones bedded on to it. If water is mixed with some of the soil it will enable the stones to be placed firmly so as to prevent subsequent sinking. Further layers of stone are added until the required height is reached.

The wall should slope slightly backwards, which means that the stones or slabs used are placed so that they are slightly higher in the front. The back of the wall should be well supported which will keep it in good position and eliminate very dry pockets since the rain will then drain into the crevices. The backward incline of the wall should slope at an angle of say one in six or one in ten. If the height is to be three feet, the fall of wall at the base will project 6in farther out than the top stones.

As a rule planting should be done as the wall is made so that the roots can be properly placed before the stones are fixed.

There are many rock garden plants which are admirably suited for cultivation on a dry or retaining wall. This is a good thing, since in most cases such walls will have been built for a specific purpose. Very often the only excuse for the creation of such a feature is to support the base of a sloping bank, and showy plants which provide colour in such places can make a tremendous difference to a garden. Besides this, many subjects revel in having their roots in the cool root run the wall provides. It is a fact that many plants which merely seem to exist in a rock garden will give a delightful display on a wall.

Another important advantage is that wall plants may be pruned well so they do not smother their neighbours. In addition, the crevices and interstices of a wall garden enable liquid manure to be applied at intervals, thus preventing the soil from becoming impoverished.

There is a tremendously wide range of suitable plants to choose from, many of which will cascade attractively down the wall. One need not hesitate to plant some of the smaller growing bulbs on the top or even in some of the pockets. Miniature narcissus, tulip species, fritillarias and scillas will prove most interesting and give an additional show when the majority of early flowering rock plants are out of colour. Pansies, primroses, polyanthus, catmint and the dwarf wallflowers will give an effective display both at the top and base of the wall.

CHAPTER 3

PATIOS,
HOME EXTENSIONS, AND GLASS PORCHES

A PAVED sitting-out area adjacent to the house is nothing new and for a long time has been referred to as a terrace, whether or not it was raised above the level of the garden. Now it is fashionable to refer to such an area as a patio, which is a Spanish word meaning an open quadrangle within the precincts of a large house, often seen in several European countries.

In Britain, a patio has come to mean a terrace or area in which there are seats, a table, various container-grown plants and often attractive paving and walling.

Many if not all patios need a certain amount of protection from wind and driving rain. There is also the question of seclusion from neighbours or passers-by. The extent of the protection and the type to be used will largely depend on the situation of the patio. Too close a barrier on all sides of a south facing site, can make the position unbearably hot in summer and lead to the scorching of plants in containers.

A fairly close hedge or a semi-open fence or wall suits most situations. As a rule, it is best to construct a patio so that it is not cut off from the surrounding garden but is part of it. Evergreen hedges are obviously the type to grow since they provide better protection in winter. Conifers are useful although a little formal, beech is valuable in that the green leaves turn to russet-brown in winter, with new green growth the following spring. Copper beech looks magnificent with its warm-coloured foliage. It is best to avoid privet although the golden type is the more attractive, but both the green and golden forms are fast growers and need a lot of cutting. In addition, they are gross feeders and have extending roots which rob the soil of nourishment for some distance around. Loniceras or honeysuckles are attractive, particularly *L. japonica aurea reticulata* with oval leaves netted by yellow veins and providing yellow flowers June to August.

One advantage with walls or fencing is that they can be erected immediately to the required height instead of having to wait for a hedge to grow. Besides this, they can be clothed with colourful climbing plants. Evergreen ceanothus, Garrya elliptica with grey-green catkins in January and February, escallonias and the variegated ivies all look well, while some of the old fashioned shrub roses add intriguing variety.

In many cases it would be a pity to cover such walls for the choice now available is extremely wide both in regard to material and patterns. Cut out blocks of coloured concrete are made in many designs including circular and hexagonal. This creates pleasing modern-looking screens, easy to erect but rather more costly than bricks.

Plain wooden fencing can be painted green or white but the paint needs renewing from time to time. Rolls of bamboo screening can be bought and this material is very serviceable and adds distinction to the garden. Then there are the translucent PVC panels which can be fastened on to timber. They certainly act as windbreaks without cutting out daylight.

ATTRACTIVE PAVING

In your patio, terrace or sitting-out place you will need attractive paving to complement the selected walling or fencing. This applies whether your patio is of considerable size, or one of more modest dimensions.

Gay-looking slabs are now available in many sizes and colours and most of the square and hexagonal slabs look more attractive if laid diagonally. Pleasing patterns can also be made by grouping the colours or blending them in a particular fashion. Whatever is decided on must be laid firm, with free drainage, and placed so that it falls away from the house. Do not use gravel or sand which can easily be trodden in.

Crazy paving is also suitable although less ornamental. It is often possible to buy broken concrete slabs but both types need careful laying so that they are level and firm. With all types of paving, pockets can be left for planting dwarf subjects such as acaena, dwarf thyme, aubrieta, sedums and saxifrage. Plants look well in fairly large areas but are not so suitable for small spaces or where it is likely that children or elderly persons may trip.

The surface of the concrete can be brushed off with plenty of water two or three hours after it has been laid, followed the next day by a much more vigorous brushing which will expose the face or colour of the aggregate. This also applies if bricks are laid down and cement used to ensure that they remain firmly in place.

A less-pleasing patio paving can be laid down by using one of the cold bitumen preparations. These are sprayed on to a firm gravel base and then covered with chippings or even shingle, but do not make a very attractive base. Neither is tarmacadam which while serviceable for wheelbarrows and other traffic, has no ornamental value.

HOME EXTENSIONS

With rising house prices, many families find themselves cramped for space yet they cannot afford to buy a larger house. This sometimes means that since the garden space available is limited, there is no room for a greenhouse which so many gardeners would very much like to have.

In such instances it is often possible to provide living space for both family and plants by extending the living-room accommodation in the form of an annexe or summer-house. Many handymen are able to build such extensions themselves but a number of firms now supply a range of sectional units, thus simplifying the undertaking.

A well-made house extension or summer-house provides sitting-out space from spring to autumn, is a useful place for children to play in and can be used to store garden furniture in winter.

Although the addition of one of these structures means an increase in rates the increased space in the house makes it well worthwhile. Many suppliers of home extensions also provide plans for submitting to the local council for building permission, as this is usually essential. Planning permission is not normally required for a summer-house not actually attached to the living accommodation so long as there is a space of at least 6ft, unless it is a really tall building or has a chimney, which is unlikely.

Home extensions make it possible to accommodate a much larger selection of plants than can be done in an ordinary living-room and one can grow such specimens as ficus, monstera, ferns, ornamental ivies, chlorophytums and *Cissus antarctica* which sometimes makes rather wandering growth. Plants with broad smooth leaves will benefit if they are rubbed with a damp sponge and a little Bio Leafshine will bring up the gloss on evergreens. The effect such plants provide with their luxuriant foliage, makes it easy to imagine one is sitting in an open garden.

It is not necessary to depend on foliage subjects since tubs, large pots and hanging baskets can be used to grow colourful flowering plants. There are many of these which although liking plenty of light, do not necessarily require full sunshine. They include primulas, geraniums, fuchsias and impatiens. Various climbing and trailing plants can also be fitted in. Among these are *Campsis radicans, Thunbergia alata,* Black Eyed Susan, *Campanula isophylla,* petunias and trailing lobelia. The range of bulbous subjects is almost unlimited, and in fact, by careful selection some species or varieties can be had in flower throughout the year.

Many plants which are normally kept in the greenhouse can be placed in the house extension for short periods in the summer. They include double begonias, saintpaulias, bromeliads, cacti and succulents. This change of surroundings will usually keep the plants in good condition and refresh them for winter.

Apart from the normal watering, an occasional fine spraying on summer evenings will be of benefit, but very little moisture will be required in winter.

A look-out should be kept for pests which are easier to eradicate before they gain hold. There are now a number of reliable systematic insecticides on the market and these are usually most effective. An occasional feed with a good organic fertiliser will greatly help in keeping the plants in healthy condition.

GLASS PORCHES

Glass porches, once a part of the older type of house are now becoming a popular feature of new premises, while many people are adding them to some of the older properties.

Not only do these porches keep the house warmer but they form miniature greenhouses making it possible to grow showy plants which give an attractive ' welcome look '. It largely depends on the aspect of the porch as to what plants can be grown. In some cases, a porch may become very hot and dry, while in others, draughts and lack of good light have to be taken into consideration when choosing plants.

Blinds can be used to provide shade from direct summer sun. Some blinds of the continental type look more cheerful and interesting than green or white shading applied to the glass.

A few quite hardy evergreen subjects such as camellias, laurustinus, conifers and some of the hardier hederas can be regarded as permanent features, but different flowering plants can be used for each season. For instance, in spring, bulbs in pots will provide

B

a colourful show. These can be followed by calceolarias, ciner-
arias, primulas and other plants from the greenhouse. Primroses
and polyanthus also look well in pots.

In summer it becomes quite a problem as to what to leave out
when decorating the porch. Certainly begonias, fuchsias,
geraniums and carnations always provide colour. Many annuals
such as schizanthus, ageratum, mignonette and nemesia produce
a show over a long period.

Among plants which will survive draughts and varying temperatures, but which need a little warmth during the coldest
periods of the year, are asparagus ferns, cissus, chlorophytum
and philodendrons. Soft-leaved plants such as maranta, gloxinia
and saintpaulia never last long in a porch.

CHAPTER 4

CONCRETE ROUND THE HOUSE

OF ALL the materials available to the practical-minded householder for improvements to his property none is more versatile or as well suited to the do-it-yourself approach, than concrete. Used properly – and using it properly is mainly a matter of common sense and good workmanship – concrete is strong, durable, economical and maintenance-free.

The possibilities for imaginative use of colour and texture are virtually limitless. So is the range of high-quality manufactured concrete products. Plain and facing wall blocks; pierced and patterned blocks of screen walls; paving slabs in an immense variety of colours, textures and shapes; precast concrete fencing in many styles; sectional structures from coal bunkers to complete garages; kerbing; drainage inspection chambers, plant containers – there's no end to it.

Concrete is easy to work with, whether you use ready-mixed concrete, mix your own, or use manufactured concrete products.

WORKING WITH CONCRETE

Besides being versatile and economical, concrete is one of the easiest materials for the do-it-yourselfer to manipulate. It does not require much in the way of specialised tools or equipment – most of the tools needed are those that a practical-minded householder will already have – and those that are needed can be quickly made up for the job or hired.

Like any material, concrete can be unkind to the slipshod worker. Scamped workmanship will show, and so will ' making good '. By the same token, it will reward the careful workman with durability, economy and appearance. Plan carefully, avoid guesswork, take your time and don't start more than you can comfortably finish, especially when working fresh concrete.

Immediately after mixing the concrete is plastic. It can be placed in position, compacted and shaped. As the hardening process continues, the mix becomes more difficult to place and work, and within about two hours – much less on a hot, dry day – it will be too stiff to use.

Once the hardening process starts it cannot be reversed or slowed; an important point to remember when using fresh concrete or mortar. Always plan the work so that the concrete can all be placed and finished while it remains workable, even if it means dividing a large job into smaller stages.

Remember, too, that concrete does not become hard by 'drying out'. Quite the opposite, in fact. If fresh concrete is allowed to dry too quickly during its early life, it will be weakened and needs protection especially in dry or windy weather.

Ready-mixed concrete is available in all but the most remote areas. It is convenient, it saves a great deal of time, effort and mess and the mix is consistent. The price per cubic metre varies from locality to locality, with the length of haul from the plant and (for smaller quantities) according to the size of the load. Most firms have a minimum charge based on a given quantity, frequently about 4 cubic yards, so ready-mix is therefore usually uneconomic for smaller jobs.

Hand mixing is really only suitable for small quantities. Prepackaged mixes cost more than the materials would if bought separately, but they save you the job of proportioning the ingredients and keep mess and clutter to a minimum.

COVERING MANHOLES

In many gardens manholes are an eyesore whether laid level with the surrounding ground or raised higher. Since they cannot be moved they have to be endured, but they can be disguised or even hidden, although they must not be entirely covered or anything used to actually fix the top in the ground.

There are a number of prostrate conifers which are of a dense spreading, but decorative habit, such as *Juniperus sabina tamariscifolia* and reference to the catalogues of specialists will reveal others equally suitable.

There are various trailing subjects too, including vincas or periwinkles, which make a light evergreen covering with purple-blue flowers. Although they will entirely hide the manhole they can be moved aside if it is necessary to raise the cover.

Lysimachia nummalaria, Creeping Jenny, with its lively foliage and yellow flowers will soon spread, as will ivy, aubrietia and *Cerastium tomentosum.* None of these should be planted too near the cover, otherwise they will be damaged if the cover needs to be lifted. Seed of climbing nasturtium could also be used as trailers.

Particularly if the manhole cover is situated in a patio or other prominent open space, it can be disguised by tubs or other containers of bulbs and bedding plants, shrubs, conifers, etc. These tubs are easily moveable and can be planted with fresh subjects every year. In fact, you can have bulbs for late winter and spring, followed by bedding subjects for flowering from June to October. The trailing petunias, lobelias and pendulous begonias are particularly useful. Careful planting will ensure that there is something of interest to be seen and in this way the unsightliness of a manhole cover will be minimised.

CHAPTER 5

HEDGES FOR BEAUTY AND UTILITY

ALL TOO often hedges are regarded as an unwanted necessity and something liable to harbour dust and pests. This is probably because the usual hedges planted in gardens are still the common privet, followed by thorn, lonicera, beech, hornbeam, yew and holly. Among points in favour of privet are that it tolerates smoke, fog and winds but not the least of the drawbacks is that it robs adjacent plants of food and moisture and often creates unwanted shade.

Pittosporum is an attractive evergreen for unexposed places, the foliage being excellent for cutting. The Portugal laurel has dark glossy bay-like leaves, while *L. rotundifolia* has lighter foliage. Holly has its virtues. It grows slowly but well in both light and heavy soil so long as it is not waterlogged. It forms an excellent barrier against animals and apart from the berrying forms there are others with variegated foliage.

Various flowering subjects can be used including *Berberis darwinii, Forsythia intermedia, euonymus,* lilac, ribes and on peaty soil, rhododendrons. Floribunda roses are also excellent as well as the various forms of *Rosa rugosa,* while I have seen splendid barriers of Lavenders Twickle Purple and Munstead Dwarf, *Cotoneaster simonsii, Mahonia aquifolia, Potentilla* ' Jackmans Var ', with yellow flowers, and *Viburnum tinus. Acer campestre* grows 6 to 9ft high. The young foliage and stems are red in spring while the leaves turn orange-red in autumn.

In an ornamental garden more attention should be given to planting coloured hedges to fit in with modern trends. After years of extensive trials it has been found that a whole range of prunus or ornamental plums can be used with entire satisfaction for producing a lively, colourful hedge. They can also be used for screening and windbreaks and instead of planting them as individual shrubs, a group or line of flowering plants can be used for garden decoration. As gardens become smaller it is a waste of space to plant dull hedges such as privet or laurel when a flowering hedge would look so much better and create a much more inviting surrounding to any property.

The deciduous prunus flowering hedging subjects are not greedy and will grow in harmony with other trees and shrubs, although the ground should be kept well cultivated and clean.

It is important to realise that no matter how quickly a hedge grows in its formative years, it is not generally advisable to allow any variety to increase its height by more than 12 to 24in annually. If it grows upwards too rapidly, it will become poor at the base and therefore less shapely.

Prunus spinosa rosea (Sloepink) forms a neat hedge of formal shape or can be trained into a garden division hedge with a round-top. It has bold bright bronze leaves which turn to bronze-brown when mature and hang into December, and pink flowers in late March or early April. Clip in early spring and trim lightly in summer if necessary. Plant 18in apart.

Prunus pissardii nigra (Blaze) is well known and has a deep purple leaf and pink flowers in spring. When the leaves drop in early December, the wood is seen to be a deep purple colour which is most attractive during the winter months. It can be trimmed into a hedge of normal shape or fashioned into one with a round top. Control by clipping in late March but do not trim in summer unless absolutely necessary.

Prunus blireinana (Pink Paradise) has double pink flowers and wine-red leaves and is ideal for an informal garden division hedge with a round top. This shape can be achieved during the formative years by pruning as required immediately after the hedge has flowered and during the summer, when strong shoots can be cut back to keep them within the proportions of the hedge as a whole.

E.M. myrobalan ' B ' (Greenglow) has bright shiny-green leaves and white flowers in spring. After leaf-drop in early December, the young wood is seen to be a bright bottle-green colour which shows up well under winter sunshine. A strong grower, the annual height increase should be limited to about 18 to 24in. If required, the hedge will eventually attain a height of some 15 to 20ft, but the height and shape can be controlled by clipping.

Prunus pissardii (Purple Flash) has white flowers and is the strongest of all these with purple leaves. It should be clipped in early spring to form a hedge of formal shape and controlled in summer as necessary. The annual height increase should not be allowed to exceed 18 to 24in. A vigorous subject which will attain a height of some 15 to 20ft. if required, it can be controlled by pruning.

Flamboyant (one Greenglow to two Purple Flash). The flamboyant effect of the purple and the green is obtained by planting one Greenglow followed by two Purple Flash and following this plan for the entire length of the hedge. For long hedges, plant two Greenglow followed by four Purple Flash and for greater lengths plant five Greenglow followed by ten Purple Flash. Very vigorous and effective.

Prunus cistena (Crimson Dwarf) is delightful but comparatively little known in gardens. It forms a dense hedge and is ideal for all formal positions. It can be used as edging on either side of paths, as a border plant for lawns or for planting around vegetable plots in the kitchen garden. Crimson Dwarf can best be controlled by light clipping in early spring and should not be allowed to increase height by more than 6in. in any one year. It produces masses of single white flowers with purple centres. The leaf is deep crimson while the growing tips are bright blood-red showing up extremely well against the sun.

CHAPTER 6

GARDENING IN TUBS AND TROUGHS

GARDENING IN tubs and other containers offers at least one great advantage over growing plants in beds and borders. You can choose the right soil and can therefore cultivate plants or shrubs that require or dislike lime and those that must have peat or leaf mould or have other special needs.

Whatever it is intended to grow and whatever plants or shrubs are chosen, some form of drainage must be provided for surplus water must be allowed to drain away freely. Many containers are wider at the top than the bottom which means a considerable amount of water is collected.

Drainage holes must be kept clear and a layer of broken pots or similar material placed at the bottom of the container will prevent the holes becoming blocked by soil. Over the crocks place a layer of rough peat or turfy loam, to stop the soil going down among the crocks.

Many plants remain in containers for years and since there is a tendency for the soil to become firm and packed preventing air and water from reaching the roots, the compost used should be fairly open. Fibrous loam, peat, leaf mould and silver sand well mixed together, make an ideal rooting medium. The addition of decayed manure or bone meal will ensure availability of feeding material over a long period.

Shrubs or trees being transferred from other containers must be placed at the right depth. This means that when planting is completed, the old ' ball ' of soil should be an inch or so below the level of the rim of the container.

Many bulbs are suitable for tub planting and where they are to be left in for some years, they can be put into position when the shrub or tree is being planted. When spring flowering bulbs go out of colour and the foliage has withered, the tub can be replanted with bedding subjects for a summer or autumn display.

Even one or two tubs of plants and flowers can make a tremendous difference to the appearance of a house and can be used to brighten the front porch and add a touch of colour to the back door, too. They bring gaiety to a dull path or driveway and since the containers themselves can be had in many shapes and designs they add to the attractiveness of the display.

Although many plants can become permanent occupants of tubs, an immediate effect can be secured by using annuals and half hardy subjects started into growth in the greenhouse. Trailing plants should always be included since they provide an air of informality. They include ivy-leaved geraniums, *Begonia pendula*, trailing lobelia, fuchsias, climbing nasturtiums which can be allowed to trail, *Phlox drummondii* and verbenas. For specific summer show, these trailing plants can be used with bushy subjects such as tuberous begonias, petunias, salvias, French marigolds, nemesias and the popular bushy geraniums and fuchsias.

Tubs can be used for tender subjects which have to be taken indoors in winter. These include the blue agapanthus, lemon-scented verbena, oleanders, bay trees, standard fuchsias and abutilon.

Many shrubs do well in tubs placed in courtyards, dull back yards, roof gardens and doorways. The dwarf Japanese azaleas such as *kurume* with its showy salmon-pink flowers, flourish in partial shade as do several other varieties such as *A. Hi-no-degiri* and *Hatsu-gini*. Camellias and rhododendrons do well in shady places so long as they are sheltered from cutting winds. *Potentilla arbuscula* has bright yellow flowers over a long period. Evergreens such as bays and conifers also bring life to dull corners.

If containers which house shrubs and other permanent subjects are turned round from time to time it will keep them of good shape and prevent that flat, one sided appearance which sometimes develops.

An unlimited variety of containers can be used for decorating the patio and other parts of the garden. These range from the rather ordinary clay pots to bowls, baskets, jardinières, jars of all sizes, barrels, tubs and purpose-made planters as well as those large crocks which were once used for preserving eggs.

This means that there is no necessity to stick to the traditional circular pots for, in keeping with modern trends, almost any container can be used. Many of these will be found stored away in lofts, cellars and sheds and long forgotten.

Containers without drainage holes should be kept in porches or under the broad eaves of houses. Those with drainage holes can be placed in the open. Wherever they are placed make sure that they stand firm particularly in windy places, although usually the weight of the compost will keep the container from moving.

In some cases they can be rested on a platform of wheels making it possible to move such containers into different positions, as when wheelbarrows are planted with ornamental subjects. While wooden tubs are most attractive they will need to be treated with a wood preservative to make them resistant to rot. Do not use creosote which has an adverse effect whether applied inside or outside the tubs. They are very useful for the modern terrace since they vary in size and shape. Apart from the traditional circular tubs, square, rectangular, triangular and even hexagonal tubs can be bought. The shapes fit in well and are in fact designed for contemporary houses. Some of the larger types are very suitable for growing shrubs, small trees and climbing subjects. The smaller sizes are ideal for bulbs and bedding plants and with proper management can be kept colourful throughout the year.

Large clay pots sometimes become discoloured by weather, algae, and mosses. Stains can be removed by using one of the proprietary moss removers or by scrubbing the pots with soapy water, but be careful if you use one of the modern detergents not to let a concentration of the liquid settle on the stems or foliage of the plants. These unglazed clay pots lose as much moisture through their sides as through the surface soil which is why they need watering more frequently than glazed pots. If the compost used in them contains peat and other humus matter loss of moisture will be less severe. To make them more ornamental for prominent places they can be painted before being used. It is these which are so often seen decorating the fronts of houses and courtyards in Italy and Spain. They are particularly useful for foliage subjects since the decoration on the pots could detract from the flowering subjects being grown.

Many of the attractive glazed ceramic pots lack drainage holes. This is overcome by placing a few stones at the bottom and then standing the unglazed container inside. The compost thus dries out much less quickly and the roots do not become waterlogged since the excess water can be tipped out of the larger containers.

In addition, containers can be moved so that they are in the sun when the plants most need it and can be moved to semi-shady places during the hottest weather.

Whereas it is sometimes difficult to site a growing plant just where you would like it in the open ground, in a pot, it can be given the perfect setting.

CHAPTER 7

MAKING A SINK GARDEN

NOWADAYS MANY plant raisers strive to produce subjects which will bear very large flowers and there is keen competition among gardeners at flower shows. It is equally true however, that miniature flowers continue as they have for many years, to hold an intriguing influence over a large number of people whether gardeners or not.

Undoubtedly there is a charm in all miniature things. Some of the very choicest of tiny plants would look lost in the open ground and this is where sink gardens may be used to great advantage, placed in shady or odd corners where they brighten a place which would otherwise be colourless and uninteresting.

In many ways a sink garden is preferable to a window-box in which one more or less has to grow plants in straight rows and follow the rather familiar pattern of having bulbs in the spring and bedding plants during the summer and autumn. With a miniature garden a tremendously wide range of fascinating subjects may be used.

The sink should be raised from the ground by a pedestal or brick piers. The glazed earthenware type is unsuitable on account of its lack of porosity but it should not be too difficult to find an old fashioned sink which will prove ideal for making a miniature garden. Since shape is not of the greatest importance, large earthenware bowls or vases can also be used effectively. The advantage of a movable garden will be quite apparent for protection can be given from an excessive amount of sun, severe frosts, or heavy rains.

Good drainage is absolutely essential and with an ordinary stone sink one outlet is sufficient, but where larger troughs are being used two are much better. With care, an additional hole can be made with a chisel and hammer, making sure to chip inwards. A piece of small mesh wire-netting placed over the holes will prevent blockage and a layer of crocks should be used to cover the bottom of the sink.

Over these place some decaying fibrous turf or similar material and then begin to add the soil mixture, which should consist of loam, sand and peat. The quantity of the latter should be increased where peat-loving subjects are being grown. Added to this mixture, should be well-decayed manure and a good sprinkling of bone meal. Rocks always help in making a garden attractive. They should be placed in position before the receptacle is filled with compost and should be so arranged as to form attractive-looking clefts and crevices. Work sufficient soil firmly around the rocks but do not round off the surface. Instead, leave it so that the soil is a little below the top of the sink.

After the plants have been put in, give the soil a covering of stone chippings which will prevent the drying out of the surface and make the plants feel at home. Little labour is required in the upkeep of the garden. In the summer watering is usually necessary once a day, sometimes more often in hot weather. Really good soakings are better than frequent sprinklings.

If a good soil mixture is used when making the sink garden it will not require replacing for three or four years, although a little bone meal or organic fertiliser worked into the surface soil each spring will encourage healthy growth.

As to the furnishing of the little garden, the range of suitable subjects is very wide indeed, and perhaps the best plan is to visit a local nursery and make a selection there. Shrubs of course are the backbone in planting, and the little junipers are ideal, particularly *J. sabina tamariscifolia*, with its rather prostrate stems. *Chamaecyparis obtusa* and its varieties, the very dwarf salix, *Daphne petraea*, various tiny *piceas*, and one or two selected *thuyas* are all shrubs worth including. There is also a wide range of very small-growing hardy plants, miniature roses, and bulbs in an amazing variety and colour, some of which will grow in any soil or aspect.

Good plants worth considering include: *Dianthus neglectus, Draba aizoides, dryas* in variety, *Erinus alpinus, Helianthemum alpestre,* miniature iris, *Myosotis rupicola, Phlox douglasii, Primula nitida rubra, Ramonda pyrenaica, Raoulia australis, Saxifraga jenkinsae* and sempervivums with their attractive rosettes of grey-green foliage. It is best to avoid the dwarf thymes and sedums since these are liable to become invasive. Perhaps it is hardly necessary to say that if one is tempted to use any plants which make a lot of growth they will soon smother the other plants and spoil the entire sink garden.

CHAPTER 8

WINDOW-BOX ROCK GARDENS

FOR THOSE who cannot obtain a stone trough or sink or have no room for one, it is quite possible to grow rock or alpine plants in a rockery 'window-box'. The plants can be grown in the same way as in a sink.

A few small pieces of porous rock placed at different angles will improve the appearance of the window-box rock garden and also be useful in allowing the plants to grow over them and give a more interesting contour. The little rocks must be placed firmly and half buried. If in the course of time rain washes some of the soil away it should be replaced. Make a few corners and interstices in which plants can grow.

For the more or less permanent window-box rock garden, there are many excellent perennial subjects which are easy to raise from seed, and which will give a good display mostly in the spring, while for the rest of the year, the foliage is quite ornamental. In addition, it is possible to sow a few annuals in between the permanent plants if colour is required later in the year.

Among the best of the rock garden subjects are the following: *Alyssum saxatile* the well-known Gold Dust; *Arabis albida*, white, a free flowering aubrieta or Rock Cress, available in many colours providing a wealth of flowers throughout spring and early summer; *Bellis perennis* the large flowered double daisy in red and white; *Campanula pusilla*, very dwarf lavender-blue flowers; *Dianthus deltoides*, the rock Pink; *Erinus Dr Hanele*, rich red; *Phlox subulata*, the dwarf Fairy phlox, lavender-blue; miniature roses such as Oakington Ruby, crimson 6 to 9in. high; *Saxifraga*, mossy and encrusted varieties; *Sempervivum arachnoideum*, the Cobweb Houseleek.

There are miniature bulbs which can be used including: anemones, chionodoxas, crocus species, *Iris reticulata*, *Narcissus bulbocodium*, *Scilla sibirica*, winter aconites and dwarf tulips.

Where space is available an actual rock garden can be made. This can be just as showy as one made in the normal garden. Drainage must be good and the general design should allow for slopes and little dells and crevices. Avoid making steep hillocks for heavy rains may wash away the soil and damage the plants.

Do not overdo the quantity of rocks and make sure that those used are firmly embedded in the soil.

Good simple compost suitable for most plants can be made up of three parts loam, one part each peat and coarse silver sand; a little charcoal which helps to keep soil sweet, and crushed brick-dust or sea-shell. Some old mortar rubble is a useful addition but should not be used where dwarf azaleas or rhododendrons are being grown. For these make up little pockets of a peaty mixture. A few stone chippings placed in the surface will prevent the soil drying out and also keep the ' collar ' of the plants dry during wet, cold weather.

Plant in autumn or spring. The general tendency of the most popular rockery plants is to bloom in the spring. In making a selection, however, try to obtain different plants which flower for a long period and at different times.

BARREL GARDENS

Where space is restricted or where there is no garden at all, barrel gardens are invaluable. They can be placed on patios to brighten dull corners, and can be painted to match the surroundings.

Get a good barrel, preferably one with holes two to two-and-a-half inches in diameter already drilled. Make sure it has not contained creosote or other substances harmful to plant life. A barrel of oak, chestnut or similar wood will last for many years. To make it waterproof it should first be given one or two under-coatings of paint.

Stand it on bricks so that water can easily run away through the holes in the bottom. Place a 6in. layer of drainage material at the base, then begin to work in the soil mixture. This should consist of three parts loam, one part leaf mould and a half part each of granulated peat and silver sand. A good handful each of bone meal, hoof and horn meal, and wood ash to each large barrel will prove helpful.

A coil of wire netting should be placed in the centre of the tub and if, as the soil reaches each ring of holes in the barrel, a small quantity of brickbat is added, this will help to diffuse moisture.

Insert the plant roots from the outside of the holes making sure the roots are spread out and the soil worked round them firmly. On reaching the top of the barrel this too can be planted.

All kinds of colour combinations can be worked out and bedding plants such as antirrhinums, asters, lobelia, petunias, phlox and geraniums look very attractive.

No elaborate aftercare is needed, although it will be necessary to ensure that the central duct is kept well supplied with water and occasional applications of liquid manure will be of tremendous help to the plants being grown.

It is however, for strawberry plants that barrel gardens are so valuable and there are a number of varieties particularly suited to this kind of culture of which Royal Sovereign and Cambridge Favourite are especially good. In addition, perpetual strawberries such as St Fiacre and Baron Solemacher are recommended. If planted between late August and early November, they should yield fruit the following year. Large-sized barrels will hold twenty-eight plants and the medium size eighteen, allowing for some on the top of the barrel.

Yet another advantage of growing strawberries in barrels is that they can easily be covered with netting to prevent birds from spoiling the fruit, while any trace of mildew can be dealt with immediately it is noticed.

CHAPTER 9

ROOFTOP GARDENS

ANYONE WHO has seen the roof gardens in London's Oxford Street and elsewhere will realise the possibilities in this method of gardening. These gardens provide a means of escape from a busy life and make it possible for the owner to grow a wide range of plants.

The making of such a garden does create some problems which however, can be overcome. The first is the effect of winds, which quickly dry out the soil making it necessary to water frequently. Something must be done in the way of providing shelter. Light lattice fencing is a help or Netlon or similar material can be erected on which to train some hardy bushy or semi-climbing subjects such as: cotoneasters; pyracanthas; *Celastrus scandens*, yellowish flowers in summer followed by orange yellow seed pods with scarlet seeds; *chaeonomeles*, the flowering Quince; and *Actinidia chinensis*, the Chinese gooseberry.

Perhaps one should first say that it is essential to ensure that the roof is strong enough to sustain a garden, as containers of soil can be really heavy. Then one should make certain that surplus water can drain away easily. A brick, concrete or even wood wall constructed round the edge of the roof will be helpful both in containing the soil and reducing the effects of winds and frost.

Plan your roof garden before you start to make it, otherwise it may end up a disorganised, uninteresting, dull place. Whether you make your roof garden on the ' floor ' or chiefly in baskets or boxes, will entail heavy work carrying up the soil. Make sure this is good and suitable for the plants and shrubs you intend to grow.

In the case of a large area, some containers can be filled with peat or sphagnum moss kept moistened, and growing plants in pots can be plunged in the material. It will be easy to replace them when they are past their best.

In many instances there will be plenty of wall space and honeysuckles, jasmines, Virginian creepers, variegated ivy and wistaria are all suitable. Climbing and rambler roses are indispensable in their wide colour range and robust foliage. In a warm corner,

C

Passion Flowers, the annual Morning Glories and *Cobaea scandens* will all cover bare walls providing interesting foliage patterns as well as flowers.

Certain shrubs and a few choice trees give an impression of permanency although of course, they may need replacing when they have become really large. Birch, maples and limes make slender trees while among evergreen shrubs it is worth growing *pieris* or the Lily-of-the-Valley tree, camellias, *Viburnum tinus*, hypericum, lavender, hebe, mahonia, berberis and cotoneaster, also laurels. Rhododendrons and evergreen azaleas are also suitable so long as they are grown in peaty, lime-free soil and are not watered with hard limey water.

Then there are a number of dwarf shrubs usually classed as conifers which can be grown. These include *Cupressus lawsoniana nana, Juniperis communis compressa, Picea excelsa dumosa* and *Pinus montana pumilo*. Suitable deciduous flowering shrubs include forsythia, leycesteria, philadelphus, ribes and potentilla. The evergreens can be planted in September and October or again in April. Deciduous subjects are transplanted from mid-October until early April according to soil and weather conditions.

CLIMBING PLANTS

Apart from those which are useful for providing wind breaks, climbing plants can become a most attractive feature in any roof garden or similar restricted place, since properly chosen, they will flourish for years in tubs and other good-sized receptacles. If there is room to plant directly into the floor of the roof garden or verandah so much the better. There are both annual and perennial subjects, the former being useful for providing quick results, while the perennials will go on for years.

While climbers can be kept upright with one or two supports they look best if allowed to spread out naturally. This not only gives them room to develop properly but the flowers are seen to advantage with less opportunity for pests to hide in thick growth.

There are various types of wall plugs and strips available from gardening stores but for climbers grown against a wall, the lattice or wire trellis work of the Netlon type is ideal. Once it is fixed, the plants can move as they will and look most natural. Where they have to be supported individually, do not place ties round the whole plant as if tying up a sack, but use a number of ties which will also help to make the supports inconspicuous. Fairly deep, rich well-drained soil is needed so that there is no question of sourness. For the perennials, planting can be done in spring or autumn. Most nurseries supply pot-grown climbers so there need be little root disturbance.

The roots should never dry out so that watering will be necessary during dry weather. As far as possible, do not plant a climber where the roots are under the eaves, otherwise they will never get the benefit of rain. It is often best to place the tub or other container a little away from the wall, and then to train the growths on to the wall. Clematis and rambler roses in particular do very well when trained against posts and pillars as well as directly against a wall. Some plants have tendrils or other means of self-support, such as the little discs produced by the *vitis* or *ampelopsis* species. Subjects without these natural aids need tying in regularly so that they remain shapely and undamaged.

Good light and sun encourage proper development but in dry positions and during periods of drought, a surface mulching of peat or leaf mould will conserve moisture and help to prevent the surface soil drying out.

While it is a mistake to cut back climbing subjects too severely, a certain amount of regular pruning is required. Old, and badly-placed shoots should be entirely removed. This is better than letting growth ramble away for some years and then drastically cutting back.

Reliable almost fool-proof climbers for the roof garden or for tubs or similar containers include the following:

Chaenomeles better known as *Cydonia japonica*. This is the ornamental quince with, according to variety, red, salmon-pink, or white flowers, which appear from February to June. Prune unwanted shoots out after flowering. An excellent subject for a north facing wall.

Clematis, a well-known hardy climber, in a wide colour range, flowers in spring and early summer. Plant in September, October or March, using well-drained but rich soil containing lime. The *jackmannii* varieties are large flowered. They should be pruned back in February to about fifteen inches from the first point of the previous season's growth. *Clematis montana*, white, and its pink form *rubens*, are small flowering and bloom on old, ripened wood. They are very strong growing and often need to be pruned quite severely after blooming. They like fairly well-drained limey soil and the base of the stems should be shaded from sun.

Forsythia, this hardy shrub flowers from February onwards. Prune after flowering, for the following season's flower buds form on new wood. *F. lynwood* is an improved form, with broad, yellow petals.

Hedera helix or Ivy, is useful because it is evergreen. It has no special cultural needs although it is useful to remove old leaves and straggling shoots in April. If the foliage becomes dusty in summer a few sprayings of water will be helpful in restoring freshness. There are several self-clinging species including *H. caewoodiana* with attractive dark green leaves, and *H. canariensis variegata* the olive-green leaves having silvery-white edgings often being flecked crimson.

Jasminum. J. officinale has star-like, scented white flowers in the spring and summer, while *J. nudiflorum* is the winter species which produces its yellow flowers during the darkest days.

Lonicera or honeysuckles are popular climbers liking good loamy soil and plenty of moisture. They do well in a semi-shady position and flower from June to early September. *L. fragrantissima* makes rather shrubby growth with scented cream coloured flowers from December to March, followed by red berries in late spring. *L. halliana* has creamy-white scented flowers from January to October. *L. belgica,* scented rose-purple and yellow flowers from May onwards. Prune old wood and thin as necessary.

Vitis inconstans or *Ampelopsis veitchii* is a self-clinging climber. An easy grower, it usually makes rapid growth. While it does not flower, the leaves assume rich autumn tints. Prune in February.

Wistaria sinensis is a favourite deciduous climber with mauve or white flowers in May and June. It likes good loamy soil and should be pruned in February. Strong shoots can be cut back to 5 or 6in. in summer. Avoid a cold windy situation.

Climbing or rambler roses are a matter of personal choice. The following are reliable: Albertine, coppery-pink; Danse de Feu, orange-red; Gloire de Dijon, gollen-orange; and Paul's Scarlet.

As something less usual, it is possible to grow loganberries against a roof wall, while if you can obtain in the early summer plants of ornamental gourds they will make an attractive display, although the heavy fruits may need some extra support. In a warm corner the Passion Flower could be grown, while the exotic-looking *Lapageria rosea* produces beautiful pink bells.

Special corners can also be found for annual climbers such as ipomaeas, *Mina lobata* and climbing nasturtiums, while *Convolvulus major* (not the weed) produces showy blue flowers throughout the summer.

CHAPTER 10

THE CHILDREN'S GARDEN

WHEN CHILDREN are part of the household their garden needs cannot be ignored. There is no reason why they should not have a portion of their own, for this fulfils two purposes. It gives them a sense of freedom, care and possession, leading to a greater interest in the other parts of the grounds.

It is of course, possible to protect the garden from the effects of children's activities by providing a concrete play area combined with a sandpit, shallow pool and other amenities, but it is a good plan to give young people a small part of the garden where they can actually grow plants of various kinds.

This has several benefits. Not only will it prevent damage to trees and plants which must occur at sometime or other, even with the most orderly activities of the young, but it encourages a real interest and respect for living plants which usually increases with age. Equally important, there is less likelihood of a special seed bed or planting area being dug up by a child's spade or other tool given for use in the sand-pit.

Do not give a child a rough, stony plot or one which is very big. A place in a good position with fairly fertile soil will give encouragement, with greater ambition for the future. Some help from an adult will be necessary for certain jobs, but most children like to work independently with their own tools. Miniature stainless steel tools will make the work involved much easier.

Sowing seeds gives pleasure to young people, especially quick-growing vegetables such as peas, beans, mustard and cress, and for flowers, calendulas, nasturtiums and other ' common ' annuals such as sweet sultan, mallows, godetia and cornflowers. Subjects with common names including love-in-a-mist, poached eggs and tassel flowers are also likely to appeal to children.

Seeds may sometimes seem to a child to be a long time germinating so a few bedding plants given in the spring will give quicker returns and help to maintain enthusiasm. French marigolds, petunias, stocks and antirrhinums are ideal for this purpose. The planting in autumn of a few of the small bulbs and corms such as crocuses, muscari and anemones will produce early colour to renew interest after the dark days of winter. One thing to remember is that when things go wrong in a child's garden, that is the time to give encouragement which will help to sustain further effort.

A patio alongside the children's garden adds greatly to the general potential for both young and old, and helps to avoid worn patches of grass which nearly always occur in summer, especially in places which have constant use as one passes in and out of the house.

Since grass is not always dry enough to play on, a paved patio not only allows the use of children's cycles, scooters, prams, etc., but if the area is used, it does ensure that the lawn as well as other parts of the garden, do not become spoiled with sunken marks.

If children see that gardening consists of more than weeding and other uninteresting chores, they are likely to become more adventurous in cultivating other subjects as they grow older.

CHAPTER 11

LAWNS; SUNDIALS

A GARDEN of any size seems incomplete without a lawn. The size of the grass area will be governed by the rest of the surroundings. Properly made it will not only be a pleasing feature in itself but will enhance the value of beds and borders of plants and shrubs.

Never lay down a lawn in a hurry as if it had to be done before the rest of the garden could take shape. It is often advisable to leave the final preparations of the lawn site until the surrounding beds have been made or even planted.

This not only makes it possible to alter the outline of the beds as necessary but prevents undue treading on the new lawn and allows time for the site to settle before grass is sown. In addition, it gives opportunity for weed seeds to develop and be removed. Furthermore, the leaving of the plot for some time after it has been turned over gives opportunity to discover and remedy any defects in the drainage of the area.

Grass must have a firm root run but this does not mean that the soil should be left unturned. Deep cultivation not only permits deep-rooting weeds to be removed but long-lasting manures and other feeding matter can be incorporated.

Such treatment allows humus forming matter, sand and clean gritty material to be added to stiff, clay soils, or manures of long-lasting character can be worked into hungry, sandy ground. Decayed animal manure and bone meal are both excellent for working in although if the lawn is made soon after a heavy dressing of manure has been used, there is always the possibility of an uneven surface developing because of the sinking of the manure as it decomposes. The addition of lime to heavy clay soil in the early stages of preparation will help to break up large clods of sticky soil but it must not be applied at the same time as manure.

It takes a good deal of time and work to establish a pleasing lawn, so plan with care and the better will be the result. The majority of lawns one sees are either square or rectangular, but it is worth considering the advantages of an irregular, informal shape. Then again a dead level lawn is right in most places but sometimes one that slopes or has a few gentle undulations has its attractions.

Tip top lawns cannot be made under trees or in full shade. The latter is not an insoluble problem but dripping from trees causes trouble and kills the grass. Some grasses will grow well under trees and these mixtures should be chosen when seed is being bought. These will not stand close cutting which is usually why they die and the turf under trees needs replacing frequently.

Where considerable levelling has to be done make sure to retain the top-soil. Then, when the initial work has been completed the fertile top spit soil can be returned and distributed over the surface. Getting a level surface is not always easy. A simple way of doing so is to drive in wooden pegs at intervals and on these place a plank of wood on top of which is placed a spirit level. Some gardeners mark out the site with pegs and string, others trust to their eyes.

As far as possible, paths should not lead directly onto a lawn, otherwise there will be much wear and tear, especially at point of entry.

It is a good deal cheaper to create a lawn from seed rather than from turf. Not only so, it is possible to obtain a mixture of grasses made up to one's own specification. Most suppliers of grass seeds have their own mixtures and will advise of their make up. To be really attractive a lawn must be uniform in texture, density, and colour with freedom from weeds. Such a sward can only be secured by using a really good, balanced seed mixture.

Always buy the best possible mixture and the one most suitable for the situation. The best grasses may cost a little more but are well worth the extra. Low grade grasses will never produce a fine lawn. It is better to sow the fine quality mixtures at a lower rate per square yard than to use cheaper grasses more extravagantly. The standard sowing rate is 2oz. per square yard. This can be reduced to 1½oz. if cost is vital. The thinner the application of seed the longer it will take for a thick, resilient turf to form. With a thin sowing, it may be necessary later to thicken up any patches which appear.

To avoid patchiness, it is wise to sow one yard at a time otherwise one may be too heavy-handed to begin with and find that no seed is left to finish the job. By this method too, fine sandy soil can be sprinkled over each square yard. This ensures even covering which could not happen by scattering the soil far and wide.

There are on the market a number of distributors for spreading seed and soil. Be careful to cover the seed thoroughly and either lightly roll the surface or better still, use a broad smooth board with which to press the soil. If this is done after each square yard is sown it will not be necessary to walk over the site. Many grass seed mixtures are treated with a bird repellent, but even so, make sure the seed is covered and not left exposed or it may dry out. The use of many of the modern bird scarers is not effective after a few days, and even in the case of netting, birds are persistent. Black cotton stretched over the area is perhaps effective but if the seed is well covered, little will be lost to birds.

Self sown annual weeds will almost certainly germinate with the grass seed. Most of these will die out after the first mowing. Before attempting to pull any weeds out, pass a light roller over the site. Then to prevent disturbing the grass too much, press down the soil with one hand and extract the weeds with the other. When the job is completed, give another light rolling provided the surface is not too sticky.

Never over-roll and as far as possible avoid watering. Water brings the roots to the surface where, in dry weather, they soon die and the lawn looks sickly. During a spell of hot dry weather it is better to give a newly sown lawn a top dressing of fine soil and moist leaf mould. This protects the roots from drought.

The first cutting is usually needed within four weeks of sowing, first scattering any worm casts which have been made. Great care is needed with the early mowing, topping the grass when it is between $2\frac{1}{2}$ and 3in. high. Make sure the blades are sharp and the grass and surface soil dry, so that the turf is not pulled up. If, and only if, you can use a scythe, this is an excellent way to give the grass its first cutting.

The best sowing times are April, early May, late August or September. In a mild autumn, the first cutting can be done in October but if germination has been slow because of dryness and cold, wait until spring.

Couch grass, other coarse grasses, and self-sown weeds, should be removed as soon as seen. Bare or thin patches can be remedied by covering them with fine soil into which seed is worked, first pricking up the patches.

Sometimes it is necessary to make a lawn from turf. The main advantage over seed is that a firm well-covered, usable lawn can be secured within a short time. One problem is in obtaining turf entirely free from weeds. This might mean a bit of searching. The lawn bed needs similar preparation to that for seed sowing, avoiding bumps and depressions. The standard size of turves is 3ft. by 1ft. making it easy to calculate the number required for a given area.

Lay them in staggered fashion so that the edges are not in a continuous line. This helps to hold them in position when rolling is done. When all turves have been laid, brush in some fine sandy soil to fill crevices between turves. Then give a light rolling but as far as possible, except in very dry weather, avoid watering newly-laid turf.

After a time lawns may need feeding but do not overdo this. Use one of the many turf conditioners on the market. These are so balanced in make up that they release a steady supply of nutrients without encouraging rapid growth followed by starvation.

If as time goes by weeds become conspicuous, use a combined lawn food and weed killer, following instructions on the container to the minutest detail. Clover can be got rid of by using one of the proprietary clover killers. Moss sometimes appears. It is often caused by poor soil and bad drainage. Lawn sand is a good control, although the moss will reappear unless the cause is removed. Remember that mercury-based preparations are dangerous to children and animals.

Although most growers will dislike anything artificial in the garden, the so-called Astroturf landscape green decor is quite useful for terraces, balconies, patios or roof gardens where it provides a fresh green-like lawn all the year round. It is pleasant to look at and to walk on, is non-slip, and is clean and comfortable. It does not rot or become affected by mildew and non-toxic fibres remain firm. It is easy to install and can be given an occasional hosing, or in the event of soil being brought on to it by footmarks, it can be brushed.

This Astroturf is most useful where grass cannot be grown and is a practical answer for all of those difficult areas needing embellishment of a grass-like appearance without problems of maintenance. It is supplied in rolls of 50ft. by 3ft. This material is also highly recommended for children's play areas and around swimming-pools.

ORNAMENTAL AND SCENTED LAWNS

A lawn greatly enhances the beauty of any garden. There are however, some places where it is difficult to establish and maintain a good grass sward. In such circumstances, it is worth giving careful consideration to the making of lawns with plants other than grasses. Some of these will grow on poor soil and not only help to smother weeds but require much less maintenance.

Thyme lawns have been known for centuries. Not the least of their attraction is that they emit a pleasant scent when walked on. Thymes are particularly good on chalky or limey soils where many grasses will not thrive. They will stand a little clipping or even mowing, in fact this encourages them to spread into very finely-leaved matted growth.

The well-known wild thyme, *Thymus serpyllum* which has purple flowers is particularly useful and may be used alone or in combination with its white, flesh-pink or red forms. Although as already indicated, these plants can be cut back when they are established, they can also be allowed to flower first so making a carpet of colour. After the flowers are over, the lawn mower can be lightly run over the plants, and this leaves a beautifully green lawn which is highly resistant to drought.

Thyme can easily be raised from seed sown either in boxes or pans of sandy soil or in the open ground. When big enough to handle the seedlings can be given more space and subsequently, they can be transferred to the lawn site and spaced at 6 to 8in. apart. Ordinary good soil is suitable and if a light dressing of organic fertiliser is first worked in it will ensure feeding matter being available for a long time. This however is not essential.

Where very small areas are concerned, especially places where it would not be very convenient to make an ordinary grass lawn, flowering lawns can be a very pleasing feature. Apart from the thymes, there are a number of plants which can be used for this purpose. They are mainly alpine in character and therefore appreciate plenty of humus matter in the soil which should be well-drained. Plenty of light is helpful but direct sunshine all the time is not essential.

Ornamental lawns can be planted at almost any time of the year since some of the plants are pot grown. When one has a few stock plants they can easily be increased by taking cuttings although, if desired, a stock can be secured by sowing seeds, but this naturally means that a longer time elapses before the plants become really effective.

Acaena microphylla produces its reddish flowers from June to August, and forms a nice spreading plant 10 to 12in. in diameter the foliage being bronzy-green. *Antennaria hyperborea* shows its bright rose flowers during May and June while *Globularia cordifolia* has blue flowers in June and July. *Mazus pumilio* displays its violet coloured flowers in July and August.

Pennyroyal or *Mentha pulegium* is a plant which has often been used for 'treading on', and is particularly useful in heavy soils while it grows well in partial shade. The rich green foliage develops into a really thick carpet which acts as a weed smotherer. It stands cutting, in fact really needs it every couple of weeks during the growing season. Another dwarf mentha or mint is *M. requienii* which has violet flowers during July and August. A further advantage with the menthas is that they will grow on banks or slopes where grass is often difficult to establish.

Other plants which are worth considering for flowering lawns are *Silene acaulis* which has rose-pink flowers from May to June, and *Veronica repens* which is particularly useful in difficult places since it develops into really good spreading plants. From May to July its blue flowers are quite attractive. Then there is *Sedum lydium* which has white flowers from June to August. It is very close-growing, rarely being more than 2in. high.

Chamomile or camomile, as it is sometimes spelt, is the name given to several plants, but the one for lawn making is *Anthemis nobilis* which has a delightful scent and is of medicinal value. The variety known as *Treneages form* is the best of all for this purpose, since it does not produce flowers and must be propagated by cuttings.

Anthemis nobilis itself was the plant used in Tudor days for making 'turf seats' and raised banks around the herb garden. Paths too, can be made of chamomile. Used in this way they are pleasing to walk on because of the 'fruity' fragrance they emit.

These plants will grow on a dry soil and remain green in drought, although naturally they do like sufficient moisture. While it is possible to purchase plants it is an expensive way of making a lawn. Seed should be sown in the spring on ground which is cleared of weeds and has been brought to a fine tilth. No fertiliser is necessary although a light dressing of bone flour 2oz. to the square yard, will be of benefit. Only the lightest covering of soil is needed. Since the seed is expensive and very tiny it is not economical to sow it on the actual lawn site. The best method is to sow on a seed bed prepared in the ordinary way and then to transplant the seedlings to the lawn site spacing them 4 to 6in. apart.

From seed sown in early March or April it should be possible to lift plants by mid-May or they may be left until the autumn. On really heavy soil, it is best to delay sowing until May or early June. Alternatively seed can be sown in boxes, the seedlings being put out during the summer months, preferably in showery weather. As with turf it is important to make the site level before planting is done, to see that the ground does not lack humus matter, and make sure that it is not badly drained.

Spacing the plants at the distance suggested means that they will meet and form a mat within a few months. After planting, give a light rolling and repeat this at intervals until the lawn is established. In order to obtain a good sward do not allow the plants to flower. The first couple of cuts should be made with the shears but once the plants are fully established a lawn mower with the blades set high may be used. Any weeds which show through the plants should be removed on sight.

Do not leave chamomile seedlings growing closely together until the autumn. They should be well-spaced out as soon as they are big enough to handle. Left too long closely-packed together as they often are in the seed rows, they tend to make woody stems instead of spreading out their runners.

The whole secret of the lawn is give the small plants every encouragement to throw out their growths and help the rootlets which form on the runners to dig themselves into the earth. It is for this reason that chamomile mixed with grass seed does not really have a chance to develop.

SUNDIALS

A sundial is among the most delightful of garden ornaments and is useful too. Properly set, it will never vary in its telling of the time, although we must always take into consideration the difference between Greenwich Mean time and Summer-time, and perhaps wireless time too!

There are two types of sundial, the horizontal or pedestal type, frequently seen set on a lawn, and the vertical type, usually placed on a south facing wall.

The dial you use should be suitable for the district in which it is proposed to use it, that is the angle the gnomon, which is the pin or shadow caster, makes with the engraved face of the dial, must be equal or nearly so, to the latitude of your own village or town. For example, the latitude of London is fifty-one degrees thirty-two minutes, Nottingham fifty-three degrees, Edinburgh fifty-six degrees. Unless you get the angle of the gnomon correct your sundial will give incorrect readings.

The gnomon, which literally means ' one who informs ', must be fixed so that it points due north, directly to the North Pole. A pocket compass will help in this connection. Remember, however, that our compasses vary from the Magnetic North by up to ten degrees west, and this changes annually. For accuracy, it is advisable to consult a local surveyor who will usually gladly give the required information.

You can then set your sundial (when the sun is shining) in the knowledge that it will constantly give you the accurate time. Almost all sundials are embellished with an inscription and it should not be difficult to trace suitable ones, preferably something a little unusual!

CHAPTER 12

THE ROCK GARDEN

A ROCK garden can be a very pleasing feature in gardens of all sizes, particularly if a little thought and attention is given to its making and preservation.

All too often the so-called rock garden is nothing more than a dump for odd pieces of stone and plants which cannot be fitted in anywhere else. Many strange objects have been used for the base of a rock garden. It is of course, often necessary to dig a hole in order to provide the proper drainage and into this all sorts of hard rubbish may be placed.

Rock gardens are now being thought of more seriously and keen gardeners realise that their primary purpose is to provide a proper and congenial siting for alpine plants. It is possible to make a very attractive rock garden which provides the conditons most likely to suit alpine plants.

Stone plays an important part but it is not essential to go in for anything that is very expensive. One of the reasons that stone is costly is the question of transport. Certainly it is advisable to use stone which is durable and not unsightly, but as far as possible, those who live in large industrial towns should avoid limestone, for the deposits of sulphuric acid and other air borne impurities cause either discolouration or very hard white crusts.

Rock stone varies in character. Among the best are those known as Westmorland, Dorset, Sussex, Somerset and York signifying from where they come. If strata lines show on the face of the stones it will be a guide to laying them.

Sandstone is of pleasing appearance and in addition is liked by plants because of its porosity. This means that they can readily absorb and retain moisture as it is released into the surrounding soil. This is a great help to alpine plants which usually like to have their roots in cool moist positions and their top growth in sunlight. Sandstone as well as other stone is often sold by the cubic yard. This amount usually weighs not much more than a ton.

Wherever a rock garden is made, drainage should be perfect for unless there is a proper disposal of water, all sorts of disorders may affect the plants. If you have a gravelly sub-soil and are making your rock garden on a slope, very little will need to be

A formal pool which breaks up an expanse of patio, and provides a refreshing sound of water on a warm day.

A natural looking pool, using a glass-fibre pool with differing depths.

Another formal pool. A four-section 'Super Aristocrat' greenhouse in the background.

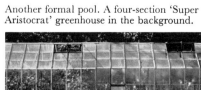

A very interesting and beautiful garden dropping
away from the house in a series of well-filled rock
gardens. Note the natural appearance of the
rock outcrops.

Dwarf wall topped with pre-cast slabs. Note the
gravel drive, not recommended too near the
house entrance.

A superb pergola with plastic-mesh netting for
roses to climb on. What a cool and fragrant
walkway this will provide when mature.

A garden frame is always useful in addition to the greenhouse. This one in trouble-free glass-fibre.

Another sauna-house with its own verandah.

Humex soil-warming equipment showing the heating element and thermostat.

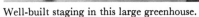

Well-built staging in this large greenhouse.

Another useful gadget.

Various thermometers; that on the right for soil temperature, the others for air temperature, and far right another type of soil thermometer with an 18″ sensor.

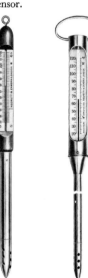

Rustproof furniture with a fern-leaf design.

A pagoda shaped sunroom that blends
particularly well with older-style property.

The height of luxury. A changing room cum sauna 'cottage' just two wet steps from the swimming pool.

'Palermo' screen wall gives a mediterranean air to a suburban garden.

Rustproof patio furniture like this can add a
touch of glamour to your terrace. Cushions can
be added for comfort when in use.

Interesting surface markings on reconstituted
stone slabs.

When laying concrete, $\frac{3}{8}''$ softwood boards divide the area into manageable portions.

Well-built steps that should last for years.

A symmetrical pattern for this path to the summerhouse.

A clean architectural pool with fish fountain
makes a cool corner on a patio. The surround of
pre-cast slabs relieved by squares of inset pebbles.

Inset pebbles again used to add interest
and texture to what could have been a
very ordinary path.

A large patio of Yorkshire paving. Note the
sunblind and slope towards the garden to ensure
adequate drainage.

done in the way of drainage. Never dig a hole or pit at the base of the intended rock garden unless there is some form of outlet for water as it drains into the soil. For preference, choose a site which is open and sunny and which is not overhung by trees, although there is nothing against having partial shade for some part of the day during the summer.

It is important to avoid a site which is draughty, for blasts of cold air can prove as harmful as waterlogged soil. Ideally, a gentle slope to the south-east should be chosen, but excepting a due east exposure, all other aspects should enable good results to be obtained.

Since a good deal of the stone should be buried, a greater quantity may be needed than at first was thought necessary. The burying of a good portion of the stone not only means it is secure, but the stone under the soil provides conditions which are liked by many plants. The stones should be set so that they will look attractive in themselves and when they eventually become clothed with plants. This means that care is needed in setting the stones individually, so that they blend with their neighbours. For preference they should tilt slightly back into the earth for natural appearance and to encourage rain water to run into the soil pockets.

If you have not previously made a rock garden make sure you have a definite plan in mind before approaching the subject. For this reason it is helpful to study some of the larger better known rock gardens where one can see plants growing in a more or less natural setting.

It might also be helpful to first re-arrange the soil and stones, so as to get the feel of the job before actually commencing in earnest. Rock stones which have stratified lines should be placed horizontally because they look better that way. If placed vertically they may split after severe frosts. The soil should be firm around each stone, and no stone should be seen with all its corners visible. Pockets and interstices will then be formed, and these in turn will provide aspects for both shade- and sun-lovers.

Deciding what type of soil to use may sometimes present a difficulty. Perhaps the main problem will be that some plants will grow well in alkaline or chalky soil while others require a neutral or even slightly acid compost. Help in this connection will be found in catalogues and reference books. It is well to remember that although lime toleraters will grow in neutral soil, lime haters will not grow where there is chalk. It is possible to have

D

soil analysed to discover its chemical qualities. As a guide, a reading on the scale of 1 – 14, given as ph7, is neutral, all readings below that figure show there is acidity. The basis of all composts is loam, and it is, therefore, important to make sure that the right quality loam is available.

A rock garden should not be completely clothed with plants from the start. Many of them will want room to develop. It is wise to get to know the habits of different species to assess the space they will ultimately need. Some are rampant growers and may soon swamp their neighbours if not kept under control.

Good rooting conditions are essential, for all plants give of their best when they have an abundant fibrous rooting system. This is always so where there is plenty of humus matter in the soil.

Leaf mould is a ready means of increasing the humus content although peat is often used too, and for this purpose the granulated form is best. Silver sand or similar clean grit plus some bone meal completes the mixture, but do not use builder's sand as this will cause the compost to cake. Usually, however, it is possible to buy a suitable soil mixture already made up, but for a large area, it will probably be cheaper to make up one's own.

It is advisable to think of the rock garden as a miniature mountain-scape where there is, or should be, a proper proportion between the plants and their surroundings. To this end, it is helpful to use dwarf conifers as a setting or outline for the smaller subjects which will be planted to complete the rock garden.

As reference to the catalogues of specialist growers will reveal, there are suitable prostrate-growing conifers which give a somewhat ragged, windswept appearance and columnar species and varieties which provide height just where it is wanted.

Great care is needed in selection of these miniature trees, since not all dwarfs are real pygmies and a wrong choice can mean that the nearby plants are smothered and the overall effect is spoiled. Avoid *Chamaecyparis fletcheri*, which is sometimes used in rock gardens. Although most attractive, it will often grow 15 to 18ft. high, making it quite out of place for the average garden.

Only a few dwarf conifers are needed and the following are most attractive and reliable. *Juniperus communis compressa* forms neat green columns. Known as the Noah's Ark these little shrubs are extremely slow-growing and specimens no more than 2ft. high may be as old as forty years or more.

Nurserymen usually grow these dwarf conifers in pots, although some are grown in the open ground. The advantage of pot-grown specimens is that they can be planted at any time of the year. None require any special treatment and once planted rarely if ever need pruning.

As a change from the junipers there are several of the *piceas* which remain very dwarf. *P. albertiana conica* is particularly good, looking really like an inverted ice-cream cone shape. After many years it will grow no taller than four feet or so and a plant supplied by a nurseryman a foot high will not take up too much room.

Chamaecyparis obtusa nana is another dwarf having fan-like growths of emerald green. *C. minima aurea* has little twisted branchlets revealing soft gold foliage edges. *C. pisifera* ' Boulevard ' is silver blue, looking its best in partial shade. It forms a bushy habit and will eventually grow 3 or 4ft. high but can be pruned.

If the catalogues of the specialist growers are consulted it may be surprising to learn what a wide range of dwarf conifers for the rock garden is available at reasonable cost.

To keep the plants in really good condition drastic action is often needed. Many subjects are naturally very free-growing and may easily take up more than their allotted space spoiling the general layout of the garden, and blotting out some of the less strong-growing and yet beautiful subjects.

Do not be afraid to cut back the top growth of plants such as aubrietia. Such treatment will encourage the development of new basal growth which produces the finest quality plants the following season.

All decaying leaves and rubbish should be removed and it is surprising how much material gathers under and around plants, harbouring slugs and other pests.

It may be necessary to introduce some fresh soil to make up places where the soil has become removed by rain or other weather conditions. This renovating of the alpine garden gives further opportunity to make additional crevices and interstices into which special plants can be placed.

The following is a selection of Alpine plants suitable for the Rock Garden, Walls, Steps and Paved paths.

Acaena microphylla. Evergreen carpeting or paving plants with bronzy foliage and crimson burrs in summer. 1½in.

Aethionema, Warley Rose. Deep rose candytuft-like foliage. Pink flowers in summer. 6in.

Alyssum saxatile compactum. Gold Dust. Yellow flowers in spring. 12in.

Androsace carnea. Rock Jasmine. Rose-coloured flowers in May. 3in.

Arabis albida. Wall Cress. Double or single white flowers. 5in.

Arenaria caespitosa. Attractive mats of green foliage with white flowers in June. 1in.

Aubrietia. Rock Cress. In named varieties of pink, purple, crimson and lavender. Most showy of spring flowering plants. 3in.

Bellis perennis. Crimson, pink, white. May to June. 5in.

Campanula pusilla. Pale blue. 3in. *C. carpatica.* Violet-blue. June to August. 5in.

Cerastium. Snow in Summer, a rampant grower, with grey trailing foliage and white blossoms.

Cotula squalida. A creeping plant with bronzy, fern-like leaves.

Dianthus deltoides. Forming neat tufts. Pink flowers. June and July. 6in.

Draba. Miniature plants forming low green tufts of yellow, white or lilac. March to May. 3in.

Dryas octopetala. Trailing plant with white, strawberry-like blooms in summer. 3in.

Erinus alpinus. Violet-purple flowers in spring. 6in.

Gentiana acaulis. Large blue trumpets. Spring and autumn. 8in. *G. sino-ornata.* Brilliant blue trumpets. August 8in. These like sun and well-drained soil. They should have moisture in summer, but kept fairly dry in winter.

Helianthemum. Sun Rose. Ideal for dry walls and banks. These sun-loving evergreens provide colour during summer. They should be well cut back after flowering. Good varieties include: Ben Heckla, terra-cotta; Ben Nevis, yellow and orange; Ben Venue, tangerine-scarlet; Bowles Primrose; and Watergate Rose, wine-red. All 6in.

Iberis sempervirens. Perennial candytuft. White. May and June. 6in.

Leontopodium alpinum. Edelweiss. Heads and stems coated with greyish 'wool'. Yellow. Summer flowering. 6in.

Linaria alpina. Of semi-trailing habit, with greyish leaves and violet, orange centred flowers. Likes light soil. 6in.

Lithospermum. Heavenly Blue. A fine blue subject. At its best during summer. Likes lime-free, peaty soil. 6in.

Mazus reptans. Creeping growth with mauve snapdragon-like flowers in summer. 1in.

Morisia hypogaea. Forming rosettes of tufted leaves with bright yellow flowers in spring. Prostrate habit.

Oxalis adenophylla. Wood Sorrel. Greyish tufts producing pink flowers from May to July. 2in.

Phlox. Dwarf varieties in many named varieties and colours including lilac, rose, blue, pink and rosy-red. 3 to 6in.

Potentilla ternata. Silky, hairy leaves and yellow flowers during June and July. 3in.

Primula. A most important group of alpine plants in many named varieties and colours. Most like a cool but moist, well-drained soil.

Ramonda nathaliae. This likes a light, sandy peaty soil and preferably a north or semi-shady aspect. The lavender flowers appear in June and July. 6in.

Raoulia australis. Forming tufts of creeping, silvery foliage.

Saponaria ocymoides. A splendid trailing plant with sheets of rich pink flowers from May to June. 6in.

Saxifraga. Rockfoil. An easily grown family of plants divided into several sections. The encrusted type form rosettes of growth, and their main time of flowering is during May and June. They are chiefly in shades of yellow, pink and red and grow about 6in. high. The mossy varieties are easily grown in well-drained soil and these again, are available in many named sorts in colours including white, yellow, pink and red, the main flowering period being during April and May. The heights vary from 4 to 6in. Another section known as *kabschia* contains some of the best species. They make small cushion-forming tufted plants the flowering being produced singly from several short branched stems.

Sedum. Stonecrop. There are innumerable varieties of this family most being easy to grow in well-drained, sandy loam in sunny positions. They vary in height from 3 to 12in. or more, although the best varieties for the rock garden are those which grow 3 to 4in., the main colours being yellow, although there are some pink sorts.

Sempervivum. House Leek. These form closely packed rosettes of fleshy leaves and produce their flowers in July. One of the best is *S. arachnoideum* of which the rosettes are covered with white ' cobwebs ' which look attractive all the year round.

Shortia. A hardy evergreen plant liking partial shade and peaty soil. *S. galacifolia* has white flowers on 3 to 6in. stems. There are also pink forms.

Silene schafta. The Catchfly. Has rosy purple flowers on 4 to 6in. stems throughout summer.

Soldanella. A beautiful little evergreen, bearing fringed flowers in spring. The best known is *S. alpina,* violet-blue on 3in. stems.

Veronica repens. A good plant for sunny rock gardens producing pale blue flowers on 2 to 3in. stems throughout summer.

Violas. Apart from the larger violas there are many small flowered species and varieties which make a splendid display on the rock garden during summer. These include *V. cornuta,* violet-purple; *V. gracilis,* violet and *V. Jackanapes,* apricot. All grow up to 6in. high.

All of these rock plants and many others will be found offered in the catalogues of specialist growers who will also give any special cultural requirements.

CHAPTER 13

ORNAMENTAL SHRUBS AND TREES

IN ALL except the smallest of gardens it is usually possible to grow a few shrubs and trees. These are permanent occupants and suitably chosen and placed, they become the backbone of the garden. They are also labour saving and properly looked after should last a lifetime.

Care is needed in order that the subjects chosen are suitable for the soil and aspect available. Height and spread needs consideration for each shrub or tree will look very different in five or ten years time. A visit to a nursery is well worth while since one can see there shrubs and trees growing under natural conditions. It is easier then to determine whether particular items are suitable for the spaces they have available.

The choice is wide in evergreen and deciduous subjects as well as those which have decorative foliage, flowers or berries. Some shrubs and trees have coloured bark, others display catkins. Colours and contrasts can be achieved especially with some of the golden-hued or glaucous-blue conifers. In the spring, the deep pink form of the Japanese cherries make a striking contrast seen against the dark foliage of hollies, euonymus or certain conifers.

There are a number of shrubs which display their beauty in winter and from which sprays of flowers can be cut for indoor decoration. In fact, if a careful choice is made, there is no need for a garden to be without colour and interest at any time of the year.

Deciduous subjects can be moved from late October to early April but evergreens transplant best in September and October, or from March to early May. Standard trees need the support of a stake and at planting time should have their roots spread out fully.

Shrubs and trees can be arranged so that they enhance not only their own beauty but emphasise the attributes of other subjects growing nearby. Properly placed, they can be used for screens or shelters to hide objects outside the garden, or to bring some distant feature into better focus. Planted against a wall, shrubs can brighten dull areas and when used to half-conceal parts of the garden, they often encourage one to discover what lies beyond;

this could be some attractive vista, bird bath, sundial or winding path.

Flowering shrubs will probably be the first choice and if these are evergreen, they are permanently effective. Ultimate size is something to consider, for although when bought a shrub may appear small, in the course of a few years it may grow to a considerable size.

Reference to the catalogues of specialist growers will reveal the wide number of choice shrubs available. We can only mention a few and any of these with good culture will give pleasure for many years and help to improve the appearance of any garden. In the list of suggestions, the figure given after the name is the approximate height in feet which one may expect the subject to have reached after six or seven years. The letter ' E ' indicates evergreens.

Abelia floribunda. 6, E. A shrub with arching stems suitable for growing against a sunny wall. Rosy-crimson flowers are produced in June and July.

Amelanchier canadensis. 6. An upright bush with snow-white flowers in April when the young leaves are a coppery colour. They change to orange-red in autumn.

Azaleas. There are many of these, both evergreen and deciduous, varying in height from $1\frac{1}{2}$ to 5 or 6ft. in a wide colour range.

Berberis. E and D. This large family contains species of greatly different habit. Some such as *B. darwinii,* 6, E, have showy orange-yellow flowers in spring, followed by plum-coloured fruit in autumn. *B. stenophylla* makes a graceful arching bush having small foliage and clusters of apricot-yellow flowers in spring. The deciduous *B. thunbergii,* $1\frac{1}{2}$, yellow, has many forms with most attractively-coloured foliage.

Camellia. $2\frac{1}{2}$-6, E. Valuable for sheltered positions, it needs partial shade and a cool well-drained lime-free soil. Many named varieties in pink, red and white.

Ceanothus. 5-8, E. Excellent for sunny walls producing sprays or heads of blue flowers in summer. *C. Gloire de Versailles* is deciduous, its sprays of powder-blue flowers showing from June to October.

Chaenomeles. 2-5, D. Often known as ' Japonica ' or Japanese Quince. Spring flowering, the colours vary from white and pink to deep crimson. Fruit is sometimes produced and this is useful for making richly-flavoured preserves.

Chimonanthus fragrans. 8, D. The Winter Sweet. Scented pale yellow flowers stained crimson, appear on bare branches in mid-winter.

Choisya ternata. 5. The Mexican Orange is an aromatic shrub producing glossy leaves and scented white blossoms in May. Needs a sheltered corner.

Cotoneaster. 1-8. This large family of mainly evergreen shrubs has many uses. *C. horizontalis*, 3, is well known as a wall plant. It forms fan-like shoots which produce a plentiful supply of scarlet berries. *C. microphylla*, 2, has pinkish-red berries. Several species make bushy, almost tree-like, growth. Among the best are *C. cornubia*, 9; *C. franchetti*, 6, and *C. wardii*, 5-6, all having showy berries.

Daphne mezereum. 3. Notable for its colourful pinkish flowers in February followed by scarlet berries in June. It flourishes in partial shade.

Enkianthus campanulatus. 5. This grows best in lime-free soil and light shade. Buff-pink flowers are produced in spring; the leaves turning to orange-scarlet in autumn.

Escallonia C.F. Ball. 6, E. This forms a tall bush with scarlet flowers from June to October.

Forsythia Lynwood. 5. This is an improvement on the older forms; with bright yellow flowers opening from late February onwards.

Hamamelis mollis. 6. The favourite Witch Hazel has hazel-like foliage and clusters of fragrant spidery yellow petals red at base in mid-winter however cold the weather.

Hebe. Previously known as Veronica, this is an excellent family of summer flowering evergreens. They have attractive foliage and succeed in all but the coldest districts. Autumn Glory, 5, E, has intense violet-blue flowers, whilst *Buxifolia*, 3, has polished green leaves and white flowers.

Hibiscus syriacus. 6. The Tree Hollyhock which flowers from August until October. It likes full sun, good soil and room to develop.

Hydrangea macrophylla. 4. This is the garden hydrangea which does best in lime-free soil and sheltered positions. There are two main classes. The Lace-Caps have flat flower heads consisting of small bluish-fertile flowers surrounded by a ring of showy sterile ones. Blue Wave and *Mariesii* are actually a pinkish shade but turn blue on acid soil or one of the bluing powders can be used. The round headed or *Hortensia* hybrids, $2\frac{1}{2}$-4, are available in many shades of pink and crimson.

Hypericum. This is St John's Wort or Rose of Sharon. The form known as *Hidcote*, 4, forms a rounded bush with saucer-shaped golden flowers from June till August.

Kalmia latifolia. 5. Flourishes in lime-free soil and produces puckered bonnet-like pink and white flowers.

Kolkwitzia amablis. 5. Known as the Beauty Bush. A graceful subject, it produces clusters of pink flowers in June.

Leycesteria formosa. 6. This handsome shrub produces a showy display with its claret-coloured bracts surrounding the small white flowers followed by purple berries. It is popularly called Granny's Curls.

Lilac. See *syringa*, the correct name.

Lonicera purpusii. 6. Forms a broad dense bush with small fragrant white flowers from February onwards. Not to be confused with the climbing forms, it can be grown near a wall.

Magnolia. This slow growing shrub or small tree is most handsome and succeeds in rich, deep soil where there is always moisture in the growing season. Good deep planting sites should be prepared, working in plenty of peat or leaf mould. There are spring and early summer flowering species. The former are the easiest to grow, flowering at an earlier age. They should be given a sheltered situation to avoid damage by late frosts or cutting winds. *M. alba superba.* 6, has pure white flowers with a faint pink flush at base. *M. lennei*, 8, has longer, thicker white petals. *M. soulangeana*, 6, is one of the best known, the white petals being flushed pink at the base. Flowering from mid-April this species can be kept small. *M. stellata*, 6, has narrow white petals. There is a pink tinted form. The early summer flowering species grow to tree-like proportions the slender branches producing slightly nodding, fragrant white flowers. These too are best planted in unexposed positions. *M. sieboldii* (or *parviflora*), 4-5, forms a small tree with cup-shaped white flowers. *M. wilsonii*, 7, is notable for its crimson anthers showing against the white, saucer-shaped scented blooms. *M. grandiflora* (Exmouth), 8, is the evergreen magnolia, its large creamy-white, scented flowers showing from early August.

Mahonia japonica or *bealii*. 5, E, is very popular since the graceful spikes of scented primrose-yellow flowers are as useful for cutting as is its attractive evergreen foliage. Partial shade and peaty soil promote good results.

Olearia haastii. 4, E, forms a rounded bush with shiny grey-green foliage and small yellow flowers in July.

Osmanthus delavayii. 5, E, produces long arching stems of wax-like foliage and in April, pure white blossoms.

Paeonia. 3-6. The tree or shrubby paeonies form sturdy specimens which deserve a place in all gardens. They do best where a fairly rich soil is available with surrounding shrubs to protect them from spring frosts. *Delavayi* hybrids have sharply cut, tinted young foliage and open their deep crimson flowers with yellow anthers in June. *P. suffruticosa* hybrids are particularly good, including Elizabeth, double salmon-pink, and *P. osiris,* rich purplish-red.

Pernettya. 3, E. The female forms of these lime-hating evergreens bear heavy clusters of berries in winter and it is necessary to have at least one male plant growing nearby. Bell's Seedlings have large dark red berries and the Davies' hybrids produce berries in many shades of pink.

Philadelphus virginal. 6, is the double Mock Orange producing large panicles of semi-double white, scented flowers.

Pieris forrestii. 5, E. Often known as andromeda, this shrub produces brilliant scarlet growths when young. These change to deep green and in spring, clusters of waxy white flowers are produced.

Potentilla farreri. 4, produces dainty fern-like foliage and buttercup-yellow flowers in summer.

Prunus triloba. 6. The upright branches are clothed in early spring with double pink rosettes before the leaves unfold.

Rhododendrons, 3-5, E. These require good peaty lime-free soil, some shade being ideal. Among the reliable named varieties are Doncaster, scarlet; Pink Pearl, soft pink; and Blue Peter, lavender-blue.

Rhus typhina. 8-10. Often known as the Stag's Horn Sumach this easily grown shrub is renowned for its autumn colour. Sandy loam suits it best.

Skimmia. 5, is a neat upright evergreen with glossy leaves and spikes of scented whitish flowers. Avoid limy soils. To ensure berrying it is advisable to plant one male and three female specimens.

Spiraea arguta. 6, often known as the Bridal Wreath, this produces in April and May arching stems of dainty white flowers.

Syringa. 6-7. Too well known to need description. There are many named varieties which are superior to the old type specimen. The doubles include Katherine Havemeyer, purple-lavender; Madame Buchner, rose shaded mauve; Madame Lemoine, white and Paul Thirion, rosy-red. In the case of single varieties Massena is purple, Souvenir de Louis Spath, wine-red and Maud Notcutt is white.

Viburnum fragrans. 6-8, E. Clusters of fragrant flowers are produced from November onwards. Pale pink in bud, they turn to white; the young foliage is shaded bronze.

Weigela florida variegata. 4. A. reliable shrub flourishing anywhere so long as the soil is good. The bright golden variegated leaves remain ornamental until October, the showy rose-pink flowers being attractive in summer.

Trees bring a sense of security and permanence to any garden and properly chosen, so that they fit in with the remainder of the surroundings, they are almost indispensable. Even where space is very limited they can be selected so that they merge naturally with other features. Evergreens prevent that bare appearance so often to be seen. Trees also provide resting places and shelter for birds.

Standards have a main stem of around $5\frac{1}{2}$ to 6ft., half standards $3\frac{1}{2}$ to $4\frac{1}{2}$ft. while 'feathered' trees are now being more widely grown. Some of these have small branches almost to ground level but not all subjects can be obtained as feathered specimens. They are useful where a screen is needed, especially as they are cheaper to buy than fully-trained standards with clear stems.

Ultimate success depends on proper soil preparation and planting and since trees remain in position for many decades, every effort should be made to treat them well in their early years.

Apart from the more usual flowering trees such as cotoneaster, laburnum, mountain ash and flowering cherries, there are other interesting subjects which deserve consideration. Pyramidal trees are always attractive and *Prunus hillieri ' Spire '*, *Betula nigra* and *Acer saccharinum ' Pyramidale '* are all reliable. Columnar trees include *Carpinus betulus ' Columnaris '* which is spire-like when young but more or less egg-shaped later. *Crataegus monogyna stricta* is a vigorous growing erect, branched tree.

Fastigiate trees include *Fagus sylvatica fastigiata, Prunus erecta* and *Sorbus commixta* of which the leaves turn to a crimson colour in autumn, while the sealing-wax-red berries are most showy.

Trees having attractive autumn coloured leaves include *Acer griseum*, the paper bark maple with red and scarlet leaves,

Liquidambar styraciflua, Prunus sargentii, Catalpa bignoniodes, Malus purpurea and *Prunus 'Trailblazer'*.

We must not forget trees which give a winter bark effect and these include *betulas, corylus, sorbus* (or Mountain Ash), *salix* in variety (willows) and *Tilia platyphyllos rubra* which is known as the red twigged lime.

There is therefore, every reason and opportunity for selecting trees which are colourful as well as useful.

CHAPTER 14

DWARF CONIFERS

ALL MINIATURE trees are attractive and those artificially dwarfed
by special growing techniques, properly referred to as Bonsai, are
greatly in demand for the living-room and greenhouse. There
are many natural dwarf species and it is these that are so valuable
for terrace tubs, window-boxes and vantage points in the garden
and house surrounds.

Many alpine plant specialists supply dwarf conifers, for these
little trees add great interest to a rock garden and give a sense of
permanence. Fortunately, these shrubs are not particular as to
soil and since they are not intended to get much bigger, the poorer
the soil, the slower the growth they make. A freshly-manured
or even rich soil is unnecessary but a peaty soil suits them
since it encourages a fibrous root system which helps to hold
them in position. They should always be planted firmly. Their
roots spread out well but become susceptible to rot in heavy
rich soils.

Because of their size, dwarf conifers will often succeed in
windy positions unsuitable for their taller relatives. Many of the
attractive blue and variegated species can be grown in partially-
shaded positions but the golden and yellowish forms should be
kept in full light so that they keep their colour. Where there is
room, they look better planted in little groups rather than being
sited separately.

The height of some, which might after some years grow up to
10ft. or more, can be kept in check by lifting and replanting every
three years or so. Where there is room for only really dwarf
specimens, care is needed in selection. Although regular hard
pruning should be avoided, a certain amount of light trimming
does no harm and in fact is necessary to keep some established
specimens shapely. It is a good plan to visit a nursery where a
range of species and varieties are grown, for in so doing one can
discover the habit, colour and general characteristics of each
one. This is often difficult to do from catalogue descriptions.

Dwarf conifers are freely available, a wide selection being
offered by specialist nurseries. Make sure to buy only from a
specialist, since in the past there has been considerable confusion

in naming. As far as cost is concerned, this is influenced by rarity and difficulty in propagation.

Some species vary greatly in height and circumference. Habit and colours are very varied and shapes can be columnar, pyramidal, globular and prostrate.

Apart from the artificially dwarfed specimens produced by special growing techniques known as Bonsai, there are species and varieties which always keep to small dimensions and which are very suitable for the alpine house, conservatory and living-room. They will also grow happily for a few years on outdoor window sills and in boxes, terrace pots and vases.

The nomenclature of dwarf conifers is rather long and complicated, the majority having no simple popular names. The figures after the names indicate ultimate height in feet, but usually this is not attained until many years after planting. If space is limited it is quite satisfactory to trim the conifers several times a year rather than making one heavy cutting.

The following are among the easiest to grow and are beautiful for terrace, tubs, window-boxes and vases as well as the open ground.

Chamaecyparis lawsoniana ellwoodii. 5-8. Upright.

C.l. midiformis, Nest Cypress. 2-3. Flat topped, spreading habit.

C.l. minima aurea. 2½-3. Twisting branchlets revealing soft golden edges.

C. obtusa ericoides. 2½-3. Rounded, attractive.

C.o. nana. 2-3. A spreading bush with flattish sprays.

C.o. nana gracilis. 3-5. Bushy, glossy green foliage.

C. pisifera Boulevard. 5-8. Lovely blue-grey. Stands cutting.

C. p. nana. Very dwarf spreading. Dwarf green foliage, hardy.

C. plumosa albopicta. 3-4½. Upright, young shoots flecked white.

C. plumosa nana (compressa). A really dwarf species.

C. p. squarrosa dumosa. 2-3. Forming a dense bush with bronzy-green foliage.

Cryptomeria japonica vilmoriniana. 2-3. Forming a neat globular bush.

Juniperus chinensis stricta. 3-4½. Pyramidal, blue-grey young foliage.

Picea glauca albertiana conica. 3-4. Conical habit.

Juniperus sabina tamariscifolia. 2. Dense spreading habit.

Theyopsis dolobrata nana. 3-6. Dense foliage turning bronze in winter.

Thuya orientalis minima. A really dwarf neat grower.

A selection from these species and varieties will provide unending interest.

ATTRACTIVE GROUND COVER PLANTS

Both shrubs and perennials provide many attractive ground cover plants. A number of these are really good weed resisters and will thrive for many years without assistance.

The ground must be cleaned before planting and weeds must be kept down by hand for the first year or two. Some weeds, such as couch grass, ground elder and mare's-tail are very persistent and it is not until the ground cover plants have formed a sufficiently sound root system and good top growth, that they become effective weed smotherers. Bare patches in any part of the garden are never pretty, and in any event soil always keeps in better condition when it is covered with vegetation.

Many low-growing shrubs are useful in their own right for making a display and for using in association with larger shrubs and trees as well as for keeping the ground covered. Among these are the following.

Cotoneaster congestus, with small dark green leaves, grows well in sun and shade, rooting as it develops. *Erica carnea* in pink and white cultivars will tolerate some lime, but these heathers are at their best in sunny situations where they produce an abundance of fibrous roots.

Euonymus fortunei has several forms which are of vigorous trailing habit, the foliage turning to attractive shades in autumn. *Genista sagittalis* is a mat forming plant with long narrow, dark green leaves. It thrives in sun or partial shade and produces golden-yellow flowers in May.

Hebe is the name given to plants formerly listed under Veronica. The following are evergreen and specially useful for underplanting larger trees and shrubs. *H. pinguifolia pagei* has blue-green foliage and white flowers, while *H. subalpina* is a splendid compact bushy plant with white flowers in summer.

Hedera. The ivies are ideal plants for ground covering and they flourish in sun or shade, on banks or under trees. *H. helix* is the common English ivy which is rapid growing, while *H.h.hibernica* is the Irish ivy with large dark green leaves.

Helianthemum. The Rock Roses are rapid growers when placed in sunny well-drained positions. *H. Wisley Pink* is particularly good and of vigorous habit with greyish leaves and soft pink flowers in summer. *Lavender Munstead Dwarf* has deep blue flowers with grey, compact foliage. *Pachysandra terminalis variegata* with silvery variegated leaves is excellent for shady conditions. *Potentilla fruticosa* and its several varieties vary in height from 4 to 18in., producing yellow or white flowers, many having grey downy leaves. *Salvia officinalis purpurescens* is the purple leaved Sage which needs sun and good drainage. *Santolina incana,* the Cotton Lavender also requires sun and good drainage. It has silver-grey leaves with bright button-like yellow flowers. *Sarcococca humilis* is a dwarf evergreen shrub of spreading habit with whitish scented flowers in winter. It grows best in shade.

There are several low growing conifers suitable for ground covering. Among these are *Juniperus horizontalis.* There are several forms of this prostrate conifer, forming more or less carpet-like growths of steely-blue. They include *Juniperus sabina tamariscifolia,* a most useful ground cover shrub with firm grey foliage and overlapping branches which build up to a height with age. *Taxus baccata repandens* is a low growing, wide spreading yew which tolerates dry shade or full sun.

Of the grasses which are useful for weed smothering, *Avena candida* forms tufts of blue-grey foliage with arching flower sprays in summer. *Luzula sylvatica marginata* has deep green leaves edged creamy-yellow. *Molinia coerulea variegata* is a choice ground cover plant with variegated yellow and green leaves and attractive flower plumes. It likes sun and good drainage.

The range of herbaceous ground cover plants is quite wide. *Bergenia cordifolia* has persistent heart-shaped leaves and heads of rose-pink flowers in spring. *Brunnera macrophylla* produces sprays of Forget-me-Not-like flowers with large green, hairy leaves. *Epimediums* grow well in sun or shade and in all types of soil. There are several species including *E. perralderianum* with dark green leaves and yellow flowers.

Hardy geraniums are among the best ground cover plants. They succeed in sun and shade and soon increase in size. There are named varieties bearing silver-pink, rose-pink or blue flowers. *Hostas* flourish in all but very dry conditions and associate well

E

with other plants. *H. sieboldiana* has large glaucous leaves and white flowers tinged lilac, in June.

Lirope muscari is a tufted plant with tall evergreen leaves and poker-like violet-mauve flowers from August onwards. *Pulmonaria augustifolia* has deep green hairy leaves and gentian-blue flowers in spring. *Stachys* Silver Carpet is notable for its silver-grey woolly leaves.

Vinca major, the well-known Periwinkle has bright blue flowers, while there is a form with creamy-white variegated leaves. These are fairly rampant growers with long runners. *Vinca minor* and its variegated form have small leaves, being most attractive when seen in groups and when used for underplanting or foliage contrast.

CHAPTER 15

ROSES

FOSSIL SPECIMENS of roses have been found in rocks in Colorado and Oregon showing there were roses in cultivation many thousands of years ago, although they were not like the roses of today. In some early records there is mention of roses with five petals and some which were hundred petalled, the latter perhaps a forerunner of the rose species we know as *R. centifolia*. The rose therefore is one of the oldest of all plants, and there are few gardens of any size whilch do not contain at least one or two specimens in the form of bushes, standards, climbers or ramblers.

Although the hybrid tea and floribunda varieties are the best known and new varieties are introduced annually, there are many rose species which must not be allowed to go out of cultivation. Fortunately roses will grow well under greatly varying conditions and there are types suited to all climatic conditions, so whether the gardener lives in town or country, given ordinary good culture, a display can be secured over a period of many months.

The dwarfer growing polyantha varieties which have largely been superseded by the floribundas, still have their uses. Then there are the miniatures which grow 6 to 12in. high and which are so useful for pot work or for border edging.

It is, however, the rose species, often referred to as shrub roses, which is so valuable in the informal garden. While some look ideal as specimens, many are at their best when used for dividing garden areas or for hedges.

R. alba. This is the white rose of York and is probably a hybrid between *R. damascena* and *R. canina*. There are several varieties in shades of pink, many reversing into a ball shape as they open. They make erect shrubby growth and in June and July produce their very fragrant flowers. Little pruning is necessary beyond the removal of badly placed and weak growths. One of the best forms is Maidens Blush with glossy foliage and full petalled flat flesh-pink blooms. *R. a. semi-plena* is a large shrub with grey leaves and double white blooms having a green centre. *R. anemonoides*. A beautiful hybrid for warm walls, with glossy foliage and single silky flesh-pink flowers fading to blush in May and June.

R. banksiae. This is an excellent rose for a warm sunny wall producing strong stems with few thorns and shiny leaves. There are separate named forms producing white or yellow flowers.

R. bourboniana. The Bourbon roses are probably of Chinese origin. They are vigorous growers with beautiful fragrant flowers chiefly in shades of red and pink. Among the best known is Kathleen Harrop which is a sport of the older *Zephyrine Drouhin.* The latter is thornless, with fragrant cerise-pink flowers, while Kathleen Harrop has light pink flowers with darker reverse. Louise Odier is an attractive Bourbon with perfectly shaped, frilly double flowers of soft pink tinted lilac.

R. bracteata. This is the Macartney rose, a sturdy climber for warm sunny walls. The single cream flowers produced throughout the summer are shown up by the neat evergreen foliage. Mermaid is probably the best in this section being a valuable sturdy climber excellent for covering walls in sheltered positions. It is semi-evergreen the leaves being glossy and attractive. The large creamy-yellow single flowers are produced in clusters from June to October, the stamens being ornamentally prominent after the petals have fallen.

R. cantabrigiensis has in May, most dainty single canary-yellow flowers borne on bushes up to 8 or 9ft. high. These are followed by inconspicuous orange fruits.

R. centifolia. This is the provence or cabbage rose much used by painters. It has large, rather lax leaves and slender flower stalks carrying double slightly drooping, fragrant soft pink flowers. It has many varieties, some of most unusual appearance. They include the following:

Black Boy, the black petals being red on the undersides. The bushy plants grow 5 to 6ft. high with strong green foliage; de Meaux makes erect slender growth up to 4ft. and produces small, flat double pink blooms; La Noblesse forms a bushy specimen, its fragrant pink flowers appearing rather later than those of the other varieties.

R. centifolia muscosa is the 'Moss Rose' which has an old world charm of its own. Growing up to 4ft. high, it has long buds beautifully 'mossed'. There are several forms of moss rose bearing flowers of different colours. One, Blanche Moreau, is particularly good. On long stalks it produces clusters of fragrant creamy-white double flowers. Crimson Moss produces globular, dark crimson-purple flowers shaded maroon. The large blooms are specially good in dry weather. William Lobb is vigorous growing, suitable for a wall. The heavily mossed flowers of purple-magenta, pass to a lighter shade.

R. chinensis is the China rose from which many of the perpetual flowering varieties have come. It is noted for its almost smooth stems and attractive foliage. All forms are scented and like shelter from strong winds. Attractive varieties include: Cecile Brunner, producing sprays of tiny, beautifully shaped flesh-pink flowers from June to October. Cramoisie Superieure has clusters of dark crimson round, double flowers. Old Blush is known as the monthly rose, the clusters of fresh silvery pink blooms being flushed crimson.

R. chinensis mutabilis makes a fine 5 or 6ft high bush for a warm position. When fully grown it is often 4 or 5ft. wide. In dry positions growth is shorter. The foliage is a coppery colour and the single yellow blooms show from June to October. These are most attractive in the bud stage since they change from orange-red to salmon and then to coppery-crimson before finally opening.

R.c. viridiflora is the green rose. It is quaint more than beautiful, for although the buds are of good shape, the actual flowers are of poor quality being tinted brown.

R. damascena, the Damask Rose is supposed to have been brought from Damascus by a Crusader. All members of the group have pale green leaves and rather nodding blooms. Among varieties are the following: Leda, the Painted Damask, having fully double flowers of blush-pink passing to almost white, the edges of the petals being tipped crimson.

Omar Khayyam has become a most famous variety being originally grown from seeds brought from the philosopher's grave in Persia. The very small grey-green leaves are downy and the small pink flowers are curiously curved and divided. Quatre Saisons, although not now easy to obtain, was once widely prized on account of its autumnal blooms. The fragrant flowers are pink in irregular shades.

Trigintipetala, this is better known as Kazanlik from the town in Bulgaria where attar of roses is manufactured. The large bushes produce clear pink semi-double flowers.

R. damascena versicolor is the York and Lancaster Rose. It forms an open bush to 6ft high, with light green foliage and loose, rather small semi-double blooms which are blush white, occasionally flaking pink, although sometimes the flowers are half white and half pink.

Rosa eglanteria is the Sweet Briar, a fragrant thorny shrub with dainty single flowers. Growing 6 to 7ft. high it is useful for rose hedges. The most notable of these are the so-called Penzance hybrid sweet briars, among which are: Amy Robsart, deep rose; Lady Penzance, coppery-salmon; Lord Penzance, buff, tinted yellow and pink; and Meg Merrilees, light rosy-crimson.

Rosa foetida (lutea) is the Austrian briar the parent of many of our modern yellow roses. No varieties in this section require much pruning. Good named varieties include Lawrence Johnston which is of rather climbing habit having lovely foliage and clusters of large-semi-double fragrant yellow flowers which bloom intermittently from May until October. Star of Persia is excellent as a wall rose, growing 6 to 7ft., the scented semi-double yellow flowers being more than 3in. in diameter.

R. gallica is the so-called Rose of Provins one of the loveliest of all types in cultivation. All varieties have neat foliage and few prickles. *R. gallica* itself has single pink flowers which are very fragrant. *R.g. officinalis* forms a low bushy shrub around 4ft. high. The rose-coloured flowers are freely produced and this is a most reliable variety.

R.g. Tuscany is the Old Velvet Rose, forming a vigorous bush with semi-double dark crimson-purple recurving petals which show up the golden stamens. *R.g. versicolor* is often known as Rosa Mundi and bears many brilliant light crimson blooms striped and splashed pink. *R. highdownensis* is a seedling from *R. moyesii* having ornamental foliage and thorns. The single crimson flowers are followed by large bottle-shaped scarlet fruit.

R. hugonis has ferny foliage and large numbers of cup-shaped scented yellow single flowers in May. This species too, has several forms.

There are many hybrid modern shrub roses well worth growing. Among these are: Elmshorn, rich pink flowers throughout summer and autumn. Heidelberg, beautiful fragrant double blood red flowers following the well shaped buds. Nymphenburg – a fine bushy plant 7 or 8ft. high with shining green foliage and large scented double orange-red flowers.

The hybrid musks are first class for specimen plants as well as for hedges; all varieties have good foliage and are smothered with sweetly musk-scented blooms in the summer and early autumn. Varieties include: Danae, creamy-yellow; Moonlight, coppery foliage, lemon-white blooms; Pax, semi-double ivory cream flowers; Penelope, semi-double salmon-pink passing to a lighter shade; Prosperity, trusses of creamy-white double flowers, and Will Scarlet, a really brilliant, scented scarlet variety which adds a touch of colour to any part of the garden.

Hybrid perpetual. These form a group of hybrids which are perpetual or recurrent blooming. They have now been outclassed or at least over-shadowed by the modern hybrid teas. Although not always easy to obtain at the present time some, including the following, are still worth growing: Frau Karl Druschki, white but scentless; General Jacqueminot, crimson, long stems; Hugh Dickson, rich red, fragrant; Mrs. John Laing, soft pink, scented; Prince Camille de Rohan, rich velvety crimson and Ulrich Brunner, a vigorous growing pillar rose. The fragant cup-shaped blooms are rosy-red fading to lilac-pink.

R. macrantha is a rather sprawling shrub with arching stems furnished with light green foliage. The fragrant, well-shaped single, blush-pink flowers open in June. It has several varieties and one, Lady Curzon is of more compact growth.

R. moschata is the Musk Rose, a very vigorous climber producing trusses of fragrant, single cream flowers followed by small red hips. This too, has a number of forms including *R.m. autumnalis* which is of better habit and produces its cream flowers from August to October.

R. moyesii is one of the best shrub roses having filigree foliage and really lovely blood-red single flowers followed by large red hips. Among its various forms are ' Geranium ' of compact growth and suitable for small gardens. Its bright red flowers and hips are most striking. ' Margaret Hilling ' is deep pink; ' Nevada ' is creamy-white often with a pink tint.

R. noisettiana and its various named forms are excellent for growing against a warm wall. Gloire de Dijon creamy-yellow; Mrs. Alfred Carrière cream tinted flesh-pink, and William Allen Richardson, scented, orange-yellow are the best known.

Rosa odorata is the Tea Rose. It is not hardy in all parts of the British Isles but it is from this species that many of the modern fragrant H.T. varieties have come. Some of these, such as the old General Schablikine, coppery-red, will give good results in sheltered positions, while Niphetos is a well-known greenhouse variety having attractive long white buds which open to large round blooms.

R. rubrifolia is grown for both foliage and flowers. The reddish stems are furnished with grey-green leaves having an undercurrent of purple. Many small single pale pink roses are produced in clusters in June. These are followed by reddish-brown hips.

Rosa rugosa is often used as a rootstock for budding named varieties. It is the named *rugosa* hybrids that are so valuable as garden plants. The stems usually growing about 6ft. high, are furnished with many glossy green leaves which change to yellow in autumn. Excellent as specimen roses the *rugosas* can be used for hedges and screens.The flowers, produced over a long period, are highly fragrant. Of most easy culture they do not require regular pruning.

Rosa rugosa varieties include: Blanc double de Coubert, long pointed buds opening to large double white flowers; Frau Dagmar Hastrup, clear rose with cream stamens and dark red hips; Roseraie de L'Hay, very large, velvety crimson-purple; Conrad F. Meyer, handsome foliage and very fragrant silvery-pink flowers from June to September and Sarah van Fleet, fragrant, semi-double clear pink flowers from June to October.

R. sempervirens Felicite et Perpetue is a vigorous rambler, almost evergreen. The clusters of crimson flushed buds open to creamy-white tinted pink.

R. spinosissima is the Burnet or Scotch Rose, notable for their dark red or black hips. There are many named forms in varying colours.

The *R. spinosissima* hybrids are really attractive. Among the best known forms are Fruhlingsgold, its many fragrant light yellow flowers appearing in May and June on graceful arching stems. Fruhlingsmorgen is particularly good, the handsome pink buds opening to cherry-pink with a pale yellow centre. They are followed by large maroon hips. Stanwell Perfection makes a thickish shrub up to 5ft. high. From June to October it produces many scented double flesh-pink flowers, which fade to white.

R. willmottiae is a graceful shrub having grey-green leaves and single rosy-mauve flowers in June.

R. xanthina is another species of bushy habit. In May and June it makes a showy display with its double yellow flowers. It is, however, the form known as *spontanea* and offered by nurserymen as Canary Bird which is so lovely. The arching branches carry many single, canary-yellow flowers up to 2½in. in diameter. The well-cut, pleasing foliage has a whitish tinge on the undersides.

Lovely as the modern hybrid tea and other forms of roses are, there is something altogether more pleasing and ' comfortable ' looking about these rose species, only some of which we have been able to mention. They deserve much wider cultivation. Many of them are centuries old, the flowers of some having been used by the great Dutch masters in their paintings. The flowers and foliage are excellent for cutting and look well arranged in all kinds of containers. When dried, the petals of the highly scented species can be used in pot pourris where their fragrance is retained over a very long period.

Garnette Roses. Anyone who has seen these roses cannot fail to have been charmed by their outstanding and distinctive appearance. They are of the floribunda type, the bushes growing between 2 and 3ft. high. Most attractive when in bud, when fully open they have the appearance of a lovely double camellia. Added to this, they last three weeks or more when cut.

Some stems carry single blooms but most produce a number of buds. If you decide to use them for cut flower purposes, take out the two or three central buds which will encourage the stems of the other buds to lengthen. Always cut Garnette roses when they are in bud.

The original and best known variety is Garnette Red but quite a lot of other colours are now in cultivation. They include rose-pink, salmon, peach, yellow, orange-scarlet and tangerine. Prune as necessary in March or very early April.

CHAPTER 16

MAKING THE MOST OF CUT FLOWERS

CUT FLOWERS for decorative purposes have long ceased to be regarded as a luxury. They are widely used, not only for anniversaries and other special occasions, but are recognised as a necessity. Even if you do not grow all your own blooms, the generous use of flowers need not be an expensive one if care and interest are taken to learn when to use particular blooms. Purchasing at random can certainly be costly at times.

Then there is the art and skill in producing a striking effect with the use of few flowers. Careful handling helps to preserve the life of blooms and this in turn, prevents the feeling that the use of flowers is extravagant.

As soon as blooms are cut or received by hand or through the post they should be placed in water. If they cannot be arranged at once, place the bottom of the stems in water so that they remain in good condition. Before arranging them clip off the bottom of each stem so that water can pass up freely. Subjects with woody stems such as chrysanthemums and stocks should be split and crushed at the base to increase powers of water absorption.

Subjects with stems which emit a milky juice such as poppies, poinsettias, heliotrope and dahlias, should have the tips of the cut stems dipped in boiling water or into an open flame to stop the flow of juice. Lilac stems should have most of their leaves removed and their ends crushed before standing them in water. Long-stemmed subjects benefit by being placed in deep water and kept in a cool, shady place for an hour or two before being arranged.

Remove all foliage from the lower part of the stem, for under water the leaves will rot and shorten the lives of the flowers by encouraging harmful bacteria. Although nothing can restore old faded blooms to their original freshness, there are ways of extending the life of cut flowers.

The placing of aspirins, pennies or sugar in the vase is believed by some people to lengthen the life of flowers. There are also a number of proprietary preparations which if added to the water are said to keep the blooms in good condition for longer, although authorities differ as to the value and effectiveness of these products. It is certainly wise to place the stems in water as soon as cut, and standing them out of sunlight and draughts is helpful in keeping the petals turgid. Although lilies, sweet peas, camellias, orchids and a few other thin-petalled flowers should not be sprayed, the appearance and lasting quality of most other popular cut flowers can be improved by very fine overhead sprayings of water.

Many subjects including antirrhinums, carnations, chrysanthemums, roses, sweet peas, irises, daffodils and tulips will continue to produce first-class blooms if the flowers are cut regularly and those that cannot be used should be cut before the seed pods form, otherwise the plants will be weakened and soon stop flowering.

It is also important to cut at the right time and this varies according to the subject being grown. For instance anemones should be gathered just as they show colour, asters immediately the petals are fully expanded, carnations before the white stamens are visible, chrysanthemums as soon as the centre has lost its green colouring, daffodils when in expanding bud, single dahlias while the central ' eye ' is still green, freesias when the bottom flower has opened, gladioli once the two lowest buds are expanding, irises as the buds begin to open, Michaelmas Daisies when several flowers on a spray are open, sweet peas when the top floret is almost open, tulips once the buds are well coloured and zinnias as soon as the full colour can be seen.

In selecting containers, try to find those which will set off the colours as well as hold the flowers comfortably, and which ' look right '. Stems can often be coaxed or coerced into position and skill in this direction comes with practice and experience.

Arrangements of flowers if cut in the bud, will need rearranging after a few days. They can be kept fresh longer by cutting off a small piece of stem every couple of days and splitting the new base to keep up a ready flow of water to the flower.

Twigs of many shrubs can often be used with cut flowers. The base of stems of these should also be cut every few days. Many of them are hard and woody so that a light crushing of the base of the stem ensures water reaching the flowers and foliage.

HARDY ANNUALS

To provide a supply of gay colourful flowers for indoor decoration or for exhibition at the flower show is not difficult if a good selection of hardy annuals is sown. These are plants which complete their cycle of growth within twelve months although this may not always be a calendar year. Some will bloom within three or four months of sowing. No special culture is required. Simply break the soil down finely and sow the seeds thinly from April onwards when soil and weather conditions are suitable.

The most inexperienced gardener will have no difficulty in securing a wealth of bloom at very little cost. While a separate border of hardy annuals looks impressive, they may be used most effectively in all parts of the garden.

However limited may be the space available there are annuals which will fit in and yield a plentiful supply of cut blooms. The fact that the seeds are cheap does not imply that the flowers they produce are inferior. One advantage they have is that entirely different varieties may be grown in successive years.

There are many interesting and colourful species and varieties rarely obtainable from the florist but which are ideal for all kinds of floral arrangements, either when used alone, or when mixed with other subjects.

Our aim now is to consider a few well-tried favourites and to bring to notice other equally good and often more exotic looking flowers which will prove decorative for both formal and informal occasions. All can be sown directly where they are to flower and all look best grown in groups rather than in straight lines.

If you have only recently acquired a garden or for various reasons have omitted to make provision for a supply of flowers during the coming summer, sowing hardy annuals will ensure that your garden and living-room will not lack colour.

Agrostemma milas produces single flowers of a delightful shade of lilac-pink on wiry stems of 2 to 3ft. *Arctotis grandis* likes sun, a warm position and good drainage. The silvery white flowers have glistening mauve centres, the foliage being covered with a fine white down. *Amaranthus caudatus*, better known as Love-lies-Bleeding has 2½ft. long amaranth-red tassels, while there is also a green form.

Calendulas are among the most reliable and serviceable of all annuals, the modern varieties being far superior to the old forms. Orange King is one of the best, having intensely double orange flowers. Radio has beautiful quilled petals, Indian Maid is orange with a dark centre, while Pacific Beauty mixed takes in a range of pastel colours.

Chrysanthemum tricolor produces a veritable riot of colour over a long period, while *Clarkia elegans* never fails to give good results. Reliable varieties include: Albatross, white; Vesuvious, orange-scarlet; and Pulchella mixed, taking in white, violet, and carmine rose.

Cornflower, of which the proper name is *centaurea*, is most adaptable in respect of soil and position. The dwarf Jubilee Gem has rich blue double flowers on 12in. stems, Snowball is pure white, and Polka Dot mixed has an attractive colour range.

Cosmos is useful where a plant of 2 to 3ft. is required; both flowers and foliage are light and elegant. Varieties include: Goldcrest, orange-yellow; Sunset, vermilion-red, and the new Psyche strain takes in a pleasing mixture of colours.

Delphinium Blue Mirror is a delightful low growing gentian-blue annual producing 1ft. spikes which last well when cut. *Euphorbia marginata*, sometimes known as Snow on the Mountains is grown chiefly for its foliage which is light green-veined and edged white, while it has bracts of the same colours.

Gaura lindheimeri exhibits graceful spikes of white and pink flowers from July to October. Godetias are popular, Scarlet Emblem being notable for its frilly single scarlet flowers. Larkspur is valuable in dwarf hyacinth-flowered forms and the tall double Stock and Giant Imperial mixtures, but these are really best sown in the autumn.

Leptosyne stillmannii produces lemon-yellow flowers in great abundance. Leptosiphon French hybrids are charming dwarf annuals each plant producing numerous 6in. stems which carry tiny single flowers spreading out in pincushion-like fashion. They are ideal for miniature arrangements and posies. *Linaria maroccana* hybrids have pretty antirrhinum-like flowers in beautiful colours on 12in. stems produced over a long period. *Linum rubrum* the reliable red Flax, has bright crimson flowers showing on 12in. stems.

Mignonette has greenish or reddish spikes. This delightfully scented annual flourishes in all soils but is at its best where lime is present.

Molucella laevis. This annual has become very popular with flower arrangers. Known as Bells of Ireland or the Shell Flower, it produces bell-like calyces of pale green. When dried for winter use, they turn a beautiful straw colour.

Nasturtiums. The older types made a lot of foliage almost hiding the flowers, but the dwarf compact Jewel Mixed growing

12 to 15in. high, has smaller leaves and produces its flowers well above the foliage making a delightful display. *Nigella* or Love-in-a-Mist is a good cut flower. Apart from Miss Jekyll, cornflower blue, the new Persian Jewels mixed takes in a range of colours including pink, carmine, mauve, lavender and purple.

Viscaria is a dainty subject with feathery foliage, producing, on 12in. stems, flowers in many soft pastel shades.

Sweet Peas are an obvious choice and the range available is extremely wide. They can be sown in autumn or spring or in warmth in February or March. Apart from the better-known Spencer varieties, the super-scented Old Fashioned strain now available is particularly valuable for indoor decoration. Although the individual florets are smaller and the petals are not waved, their daintiness and perfume make them almost essential for indoor decoration.

Ornamental grasses and even the decorative cabbages and Kales, can also play a part in creating a worthwhile display, both in the garden and in the living-room.

BIENNIALS

These are plants raised from seed for flowering the following season, after which they die. Quite a number of perennials are treated as biennials because they do not stand a second winter well. Even if they are not killed, they become so shabby that they either fail to recover or if they do, they never give a satisfactory display. They include antirrhinums, Sweet Williams, gaillardias and Wallflowers.

Seeds of biennials should be sown in May, June or early July. A well-prepared seed bed should be made, but avoid nitrogenous fertilisers since these often lead to soft, sappy growth, susceptible to cold damage. Thin them out early so they make bushy specimens. The aim should be to have the plants in their flowering positions by the end of October so they become established before severe weather.

The following are among the most reliable biennials, or perennials treated as biennials. All give a rewarding display under good growing conditions.

Brompton Stocks are always popular. Select a warm corner for them or cover with cloches in very severe weather to give protection from both cold and damp. Early thinning before moving them to flowering positions promotes a fibrous root system. While a mixture is usually grown, separate colours such as crimson, rose, mauve and white are available, all on 18in. stems. The East Lothian or Intermediate stocks, 15in., can be treated similarly, but they do best when protected during the winter. Excellent for cutting, these too can be had in a mixture or in separate colours.

Canterbury Bells are old favourites and are delightful for an early summer display in the garden or for cutting. Growing up to 3ft. high, they are valuable where tall stems are needed. To ensure thin sowing, the tiny seed can be mixed with sand. Apart from the single and double forms, the Cup and Saucer varieties in blue, pink and white are most attractive.

Cheiranthus allionii will sometimes come through a second winter. Often known as Siberian Wallflower, this is an excellent bedding plant whose brilliant orange flowers are continuously produced. Golden Bedder is rich golden-yellow, and the lesser known *C. linifolius* is mauve.

Cheiranthus cheri is the botanical name of the plants we know best as Wallflowers. These are definitely perennial plants. They like well-drained soil but are susceptible to club root, so that a well-limed position should be selected for growing the plants. Firm planting is essential and this combined with the pinching out of the growing points, will encourage side shoots to develop.

The range of varieties is wide, as will be seen on reference to seedsmen's catalogues. The following are most reliable cultivars making excellent cut blooms with pleasing fragrance.

Blood Red, deep crimson; Cloth of Gold, bright yellow; Eastern Queen, apricot changing to bright red; Fire King, brilliant orange; Ivory White, creamy-white; Orange Bedder, orange-apricot; Ruby Gem, ruby-violet; Vulcan, velvety-crimson; and Scarlet Emperor, pure scarlet.

In addition, there are first class mixtures including: Monarch Fair Lady, 1ft.; and Tom Thumb, 9in. Less common is the double mixed, growing 1½ft. high.

Cut the spikes when several of the lower flowers are open and with the stems as long as possible. The lower leaves should be stripped off the base of the stems. This will prevent fouling of the water.

Cynoglossum amabile is particularly useful because of the colour of its pleasing mid-blue flowers produced on 2ft. stems which are so useful for including in formal and informal flower arrangements.

Digitalis. This native of Britain is familiarly known as Foxglove. From the original *D. purpurea* which has purple flowers, have come a number of selections many with beautifully spotted trumpets as well as the Excelsior strain which produces florets all round the 4 to 5ft. stems. An even newer variety, Foxy, will actually flower the same year if sown in boxes in March. Growing only 3ft. high, the compact plants produce a varied range of spotted flowers.

Hesperis matronalis is best known as Sweet Rocket, while another common name is Dame's Violet. It is somewhat like a Stock in appearance, the toothed leaves being hairy. On 2½ to 3ft. stems, the plants produce violet-lilac or white flowers. The name *hesperis* comes from the Greek *hespera* meaning evening, at which time during June and July, the flowers are most fragrant. Sow the seed in May or June in prepared beds of good soil which will remain moist. Select a light soil which does not dry out and before the plants are moved to their final positions in early autumn, a dusting of lime will be helpful. The flowers need to be treated carefully when cut, for if the stems are not placed in water immediately, they are likely to wilt quickly and prove disappointing.

Lunaria biennis. This plant is widely known as Honesty and in some parts of the country it is referred to as Moonwort because of the shape of the seed vessels. An erect growing plant, it produces broad, pointed leaves and 3ft. branching spikes of mauve flowers which open in May and June. Seeds are sown in prepared beds of good, but not over rich soil in May, the plants being moved to their flowering quarters in August or early September. Allow at least a foot between the plants. Cut the spikes in autumn, when the seed pods have formed. If the outer skins are removed, the glistening transparent white ' moons ' will be revealed. They look admirable used in an arrangement of leaves and autumn flowers.

There are several varieties, the most popular being Munstead Purple. Other colours include white, mauve and crimson.

Myosotis, the well-known Forget-me-Not, has long been grown in British gardens. There are a number of species and although some are perennials they are not reliably hardy and even when they come through the winter, they are usually very untidy looking. It is therefore best to sow annually. The main trouble with many of them is that they seed so freely dropping their seed all round the plants so that self-sown seedlings quickly lose their distinctive character. Thin out the seedlings before they become crowded and weak and move the plants to their flowering places in October or early November. *Myosotis* like positions where they never lack moisture and succeed in partial shade although they flower more abundantly in sunny situations. The naming of Forget-me-Nots is somewhat confusing. In seed catalogues they are usually offered as *Myosotis alpestris* or *sylvatica* cultivars such as Victoria, bright blue; Marine, mid-blue; both 6-7in.; Royal Blue, indigo blue and Carmine King, rosy-carmine grow 10 to 12in. *M. palustris* the water Forget-me-Not is useful for growing in wet ground or at the edges of ponds or streams.

Sweet William. These members of the dianthus family are really perennials, but are best treated as biennials, since they become straggly and in poor condition after cold weather. In warm, sheltered positions the plants come through the winter reasonably well. Seedlings should be transplanted to beds, allowing 8 or 9in. between the plants so that they do not become drawn and weak. Subsequently move them to their flowering positions not later than the end of October. Ordinary good soil is quite suitable although lime is liked. Good named varieties available, including Scarlet Beauty, Pink Beauty and Dunnett's Deep Crimson, the latter having dark foliage as well as flowers. The auricula-eyed mixture is old fashioned but still very attractive. A newer strain known as Messenger mixed, flowers fourteen days earlier than the older types and has a rich, bright colour range. All of these grow 1½ to 2ft. high, although often they remain about 18in.

The dwarf double mixed are quite distinct, rarely growing more than 10in. high. They form compact, uniform plants and during June and July produce 60 to 70 per cent double flowers in a bright and effective colour range.

PERENNIALS

The popularity of hardy perennials is in no small way due to their being permanent members of the garden. One can be reasonably sure of their annual appearance especially if the plants are lifted and divided every three years. With proper selection they rarely suffer from the effects of the most severe winter. Most will flourish in ordinary good soil and when making a new bed or border it is helpful to work in plenty of humus-forming matter such as decayed manure, compost, peat, leaf mould, hop manure, plus some bone meal.

F

Planting can be done in autumn or spring, although some items such as Scabious are best moved only in spring. Best effects are obtained by grouping perennial plants in threes rather than dotting them singly about the border. It is advisable to use plants with upright foliage such as irises and kniphofias near those with wider lower foliage, for the latter produce a steadying base to the border.

Contrasts and harmonies can be worked out not only in the colour of the flowers but in the many shades of green and differently coloured and variegated foliage. I see no valid objection to including a few well-chosen shrubs in the border, for often they provide the backbone or skeleton around which perennial plants can be placed.

While we can mention only a few of the many first-class plants worthy of a place in the cut flower section of the garden, the following ought not to be overlooked. *Acanthus mollis* is known as Bears Breeches having leaves 2ft. long and purple and white flowers shaped like dragons' heads. *A. spinosus* has deeply cut leaves with prominent sharp, white spines. *Achillea eupatorium (filipendulina)* grows up to 5ft. high producing many flat yellow heads of flowers. Gold Plate is a newer form, while Coronation Gold is shorter growing. *A. ptarmica*, The Pearl, produces buttonlike white flowers. Easy to grow, it is best divided and replanted every two years.

Aconitum is a tall late summer flowering subject of similar appearance to the delphinium. Newry Blue and Spark's variety have fine blue flowers while *A. napellus bicolor* is blue and white.

Anthemis Grallagh Gold, and Mrs. E. C. Buxton produce masses of yellow daisy-like flowers in season.

Aster. The perennial varieties are of widely different appearance. Particularly good are the amellus varieties, such as King George, lavender-blue. Small flowering kinds such as *A. cordifolius* and *A. ericoides* are most effective for their dainty appearance when mixed with other flowers. The *A. novi-belgii* varieties are the most widely grown and usually referred to as Michaelmas Daisies. Among good varieties are: Eventide, deep blue; Marie Ballard, powder-blue; Fellowship, soft pink; Crimson Brocade, ruby-red and Royal Velvet, violet.

Campanula glomerata dahurica is an old fashioned, comfortable looking plant growing $2\frac{1}{2}$ to 3ft. high. During June and July it produces heads of violet-blue flowers. *C. persicifolia* has slender stems of 3ft. or so carrying several open cupped flowers from June to August.

Fleur de Neige is double blue, while Pride of Exmouth is light blue, and Telham Beauty, a single light blue.

Cephalaria tartarica is the giant yellow Scabious. It grows 5 to 6ft. high producing many light yellow heads over a long period in summer.

Chrysanthemum maximum is first class as a lasting cut flower. The double forms are particularly useful. Among these are: Esther Read and Wirral Supreme double white; Jenifer Read has a yellowish centre, and Cobham Gold flushed yellow. *C. rubellum* is a true hardy perennial producing single, yellow disced, rayed flowers in abundance through the summer. There are many named varieties in shades of pink, yellow bronze and apricot.

Coreopsis grandiflora is another old established cut flower favourite. The pretty yellow flowers on 2ft. wiry stems are long lasting, the varieties Mayfield Giant and Badengold being particularly good. *C. verticillata* produces many one inch golden-yellow starry flowers on 1½ to 2ft. stems.

Delphiniums are not used as cut flowers as widely as they deserve, probably because they are rather formal looking. In large arrangements, the spikes give an essential towering line, while they make a splendid decoration placed in containers on the floor. There are many named varieties some with dark centres. The Pacific Giant strain takes in shades of blue, pink, lilac and white, some with a dark central ' bee '. The Belladonna delphiniums are daintier, growing 2½ to 3½ft. high.

Dianthus allwoodii pinks are excellent for cutting. They like sun and well-drained soil. Part of their attraction is their lovely perfume. Among the best of the doubles is Monty, orange-scarlet; and good varieties in shades of pink and red, are Rupert, Betty, Derek and Eva. Winston is a fine red single, and Yellow Hammer is noteworthy because of its colour.

Dicentra spectabilis is the Bleeding Heart. It has well cut ferny foliage and 2ft. arching sprays of pendant rose-pink flowers from May to July.

Doronicum plantagineum excelsum ' Harper Crewe ' produces in early spring, yellow daisy-like flowers on 2½ft. stems. It flourishes in good soil which never dries out.

Echinops or Globe Thistles like a sunny situation in good deep soil since the roots penetrate deeply. The metallic-blue heads develop in summer and are long lasting. *E. ritro* grows 3ft. and Taplow Purple, 4 to 4½ft. high.

Eryngium is the Sea Holly so useful for drying for Christmas decoration. *E. planum*, 2½ft., has steel blue, cone-shaped heads while *E. tripartitum*, 4ft., makes really bold plants.

Gaillardia grandiflora has long been grown as a cut flower plant. It likes sun and good drainage. There are a number of good varieties all growing 2½ to 3ft. high. They include Burgundy, reddish-brown; Ipswich Beauty, yellow and crimson; and Wirral Flame, flame-mahogany with yellow tips.

Geums are old favourites and grow well in sun or partial shade. Good varieties are Lady Stratheden, yellow; Mrs. Bradshaw, scarlet, and Fire Opal, orange-red, all flowering from June to August on 18 to 24in. stems.

Gypsophila paniculata is first class for ' mixing ' with other cut flowers. The large branching 4ft. high sprays of white flowers appearing in summer, are very dainty. The double form, Bristol Fairy, is the most popular.

The *Heleniums* are long lasting subjects which like the sun. They will reward good treatment with a plentiful supply of blooms. The colours range from yellow to brownish-red and according to variety they flower from June to September. Particularly good are Chipperfield Orange 4 to 5ft., reddish-brown; Crimson Beauty, 2ft., brownish-red; Mme. Canivet, 3ft., golden-yellow, and Moerheim Beauty, 2½ft., brown shaded orange-red.

Helianthus. The Sunflower family is very large and those most useful as cut flowers include: *H. scaber* (or *rigidus*) 4ft., yellow with brown disc, Soleil d'Or, 5ft., double yellow, and *Sparsifolius*, 5½ft., semi-double orange. All show colour from late June onwards. Plunge the stems in water as soon as they are cut. They will then last a long time.

Heliopsis. This subject produces strong stems and many golden-yellow flowers often as much as 3 or 4in. in diameter. *H. incomparabilis*, 3ft., is of branching habit, other good varieties being *H. palula* and *H. gigantea*.

Helleborus. This most useful subject flourishes where the soil does not dry out. Deep loamy soil containing leaf mould is ideal, while light shade is no drawback. *H. niger* is the white Christmas Rose of which there are several forms some having petals stained green or pink. To prevent the petals being marked by soil splashings or severe weather, cover them in December with cloches or place straw around the plants. *H. orientalis* is the Lenten Rose of which there are many named varieties flowering from late February onwards. The colour range is wide, many being prettily spotted.

Heuchera is a very dainty easy to grow cut flower producing 15 to 24in. spikes of feathery flowers on strong stems. *H. brizoides,* rose-carmine, *H. gracillima,* rosy-crimson, and *H. sanguinea,* Edge Hall are particularly good forms.

Inula produces yellow daisy-like flowers on 18in. stems throughout the summer. Good species include *I. glandulosa* and *I. royleana.*

Kniphofias or Red Hot Pokers are useful where spiky cut flowers are needed. They like a situation where the soil does not dry out. *K. aloides* produces orange-scarlet pokers from July to September. *K. goldelse* is soft yellow, *K. galpinii,* apricot-orange often going on until November, and *K. macowanii* is coral red.

Liatris has the common name of Snakeroot. The erect growing flower stems are clothed with smallish leaves. All flower from early August to late September. *L. callilapis,* magenta-purple, *L. punctata,* violet-purple and *L. pycnostachya* are good. The last named is popular with florists.

Limonium latifolia is often known as the perennial Statice. The sprays of lavender-blue flowers are long lasting, and are often dried and used for winter decoration.

Iris. This large family contains many different species and varieties. *Iris germanica* is the Flag Iris, and probably the most popular of all. The colour range is very wide indeed. Apart from the many art shades and the striped or flushed sorts, there are some which give a plush looking effect, the colours being mulberry, deep strawberry red or maroon-red.

It is some of the smaller growing irises that are specially good for cutting. *I. graminea* grows 15 to 20in. high and in May and June, produces violet-purple scented flowers with purplish markings on a white ground. *I. ruthenica,* 6 to 9in. high, shows its fragrant blue flowers in April, while *I. tectorum* has striking flattish blue blooms in May and June on 2ft. stems. *I. longipetala,* 2ft., lavender-blue reticulated white, and *I. innominata,* 9in., produces grass-like foliage and buttercup-yellow flowers.

Monarda, often known as Bergamot or Bee Balm, makes 2½ to 3ft. bushes of aromatic foliage topped by curious honeysuckle-shaped flowers which appear over a long period in summer. Partial shade, where the soil does not dry out suits these plants. M. Cambridge Scarlet and Croftway Pink are first class, while there are several hybrids in shades of pink, purple and mahogany.

Nepeta, often referred to as Catmint, is useful where spikes of lavender-blue are required in June and July. *N. tartarica*, 2½ft., is strong growing but *N. faassenii*, better known as *N. mussinii*, is daintier but rather spreading.

Paeonies. These are very long lasting as cut flowers. They flourish in deep well-drained soil, preferably in a sunny position. Liberal feeding with liquid manure leads to better, firmer textured petals. The early foliage is beautifully coloured, while after flowering, the leaves take on autumn tints. There are single and double varieties in many colours.

Papaver nudicaule, the Iceland Poppy, is best treated as a biennial. The colour range is wide, taking in shades of red, orange, salmon, yellow, chamois and white. It is essential to cut the flowers just as the petals show colour through the green sepals. To ensure that they do not flag, dip the ends of the stems in boiling water for a few seconds, or hold them over a flame.

Papaver orientale is the Oriental Poppy which shows its large flowers during May and June. Good named varieties are available in choice colours, most having a shiny, embossed black centre. Cut the flowers just as the buds split and the petals look like crumpled satin.

Phygelius capensis, the Cape Figwort, is a handsome plant for those who like something out of the ordinary. If placed near a fence or wall, it grows up to 4 or 5ft. high; in the open ground, it usually reaches 3ft. Sometimes cut down by severe spring frosts, it soon makes fresh basal growths. It produces graceful tubular, crimson-scarlet flowers from June to September.

Physostegia virginiana, Vivid, has 2½ft. leafy spikes of closely set tubular pink flowers. A curious feature of this plant is that the individual flowers remain in whatever position they are moved to on the stem.

Pinks are old fashioned flowers of the easiest culture. They do best in soil containing lime, and bloom profusely over a long time. Mrs. Sinkins is the best known, while White Ladies is a large variety. Inchmery is pale pink, and Dad's Favourite is white with chocolate edging.

Polygonatum multiforum is Solomon's Seal, useful for its 2 to 3ft. leafy arching stems of greenish-white bells. It likes cool root conditions and can become a feature in a shady corner. *Poly-*

Polygonatum—Solomon's Seal.

gonum bistorta superbum, produces brush-like heads of reddish flowers on 18 to 24in. wiry stems. *P. amplexicaule* is taller and flowers in autumn.

Polyanthus. Several modern strains are ideal for cutting since they have long, strong stems. Apart from the more usual mixtures, Pacific Giant Blue, and the mixture, are particularly good, while

Greensleeves, taking in shades of pale green, lime green and creamy-green is greatly valued by flower arrangers.

Pyrethrums are among the most popular spring flowering cut blooms. They do best in rather light soil which should not dry out in summer. They like good root conditions but too much feeding may lead to weak stems which bend easily. Dividing the plants after the flowering periods means that the new plants soon become established. There are single and double named varieties in shades of pink, red and white.

Ranunculus. Apart from the tuberous rooted species there are a number of herbaceous kinds which are useful for cutting. They include: *R. acris plenus* with double, yellow button-like flowers. *R. speciosum plenus* has larger flowers on rather shorter stems. They succeed in ordinary soil which does not dry out.

Rudbeckia. Some of these will last up to a week when placed in water. *R. newmanii* and *R. deanii* Goldsturn have yellow petals and black centres. *R. laciniata* Golden Glow, is good as is the dwarfer Goldquelle.

Scabiosa is one of the most widely grown cut flowers. It not only lasts well in water but the plants bloom over a long period beginning in June. The plants flourish in any good soil so long as it contains lime. Faded flowers should be removed before they seed. Clive Greaves is the most popular variety, its delicate mauve flowers on 2ft. stems looking well on their own, or seen with other subjects. There are several different kinds in shades of blue or mauve while Miss Willmott is creamy-white.

Sedum spectabile, 15 to 18in., produces heads of rose-red flowers in late summer and early autumn. Plants also look well in pots.

Solidago. The taller Golden Rods are liable to become a nuisance. There are now a number of dwarfer varieties including Golden Mosa and Lemore both about 2ft. high, with elegant heads of rich yellow.

Stokesia cyanea produces lavender-blue, aster-like flowers as much as 3in. in diameter. These appear on 18in. stems from August to October making them valuable as late flowers especially since they last well when cut.

Thalictrum. This is a most attractive plant when seen growing and when the flowers are cut. Not difficult to cultivate, it likes a sunny situation and good deep soil.

T. dipterocarpum is probably the best species. It grows $4\frac{1}{2}$ to 6ft.

high and looks best when staked. The well shaped bushy plants produce throughout the summer, graceful sprays of lavender-mauve single flowers each having prominent yellow stamens. The finely cut foliage adds to its value. The form known as Hewitts Double is even better, its sprays of small violet-pink flowers being carried on dainty but strong stems. There is a less common form known as album, having double white, pearl-like flowers.

Trollius is useful since it flowers freely in May and June. It flourishes in humus-rich moisture holding soil. The best varieties for cutting are T. Orange Princess 1½ft., and Golden Queen, 2ft.

No cut flower plants should be allowed to run to seed for this weakens them. Remove the heads once the petals have faded.

CUT FLOWERS FROM BULBS

By careful selection and planning it is possible to secure flowers from outdoor bulbous subjects throughout the whole year. No special culture is needed although good well-drained soil not lacking in nourishment or humus matter will encourage the most prolific results.

Alstromerias are tuberous rooted perennials of elegance. They produce umbels of semi-funnel shaped flowers on wiry stems of 2ft. Apart from the well-known orange coloured varieties, the Ligtu hybrids are superb. These produce flowers in shades of pink, flame, orange and yellow.

Acidantheras make strong spikes reaching a height of 2½ to 3ft., the large flowers being of the purest silver-white, all except the top petal which is marked with a conspicuous deep maroon blotch near the centre, while the foliage is typically that of a gladiolus, although a little narrower. Not the least of the attributes of this delightful plant is the fact that it continues to bloom over a long period and it is not unusual to be able to cut blooms from the end of July until well into October.

Brodiaea laxa produces in June, wide mouthed tubular flowers, sumptuous violet-purple in colour with blue anthers. The stems are very stiff and sturdy and some are 18in. tall. It is an excellent cut flower in June.

Calochortus are sometimes known as Mariposa or Butterfly tulips, whilst certain varieties have been described as Star or Globe tulips. They come chiefly from California, and their light, graceful growth and charming brightly coloured flowers, make them altogether attractive and very valuable for cutting.

Freesia. The delicate pastel freesias of remarkable fragrance available in florists' shops can be grown in your own garden. Specially prepared corms for outdoor cultivation are available in a glorious rainbow mixture. By planting corms from mid-April you can have an abundance of elegant flowers in your garden from late July to October. They thrive in average garden loam which is well worked over, and like sunny, sheltered positions. Plant the corms about 2in. deep and 2 to 3in. apart, remembering to water them regularly in dry weather, particularly during the early growing stages.

Galanthus or Snowdrops should be planted as available in September or October, about 4in. deep in light soils and 6in. in heavy soils. They flourish in fairly solid, damp, heavy soil.

Galanthus nivalis is the common or classic Snowdrop species of European origin. Naturalised, they form vast white carpets as early as January. *G. nivalis flore-pleno* is an exquisite double form with large globular blooms. Both have 6in. tall stems.

For a riot of colour in the garden and a succession of spikes for cutting, few flowers compare with *gladiolus*, universal leader of the summer flowering bulbs. The successful cultivation of all types is the same. Almost any soil will do, but to produce the best spikes and flowers, soil should be well enriched and also contain plenty of humus, supplied by compost, organic matter or peat. Always prepare the ground well in advance, digging at least 8in. deep and working in 3oz. of a complete garden fertiliser per square yard. Do remember that gladiolus do not like freshly manured ground but soil manured for a previous crop is ideal.

Varieties of gladiolus are legion, varying from the sturdy Large Flowered varieties to the dainty Primulinus sorts. There are several other kinds such as Butterfly, Miniature and the Early Flowering varieties which can be planted in pots in the greenhouse in the autumn and which are so dainty with their reflexing petals. The colours extend from the palest art shades to the rich crimson and maroon tones.

Irises. This name means rainbow, an indication of the wide colour range in the family. Dutch irises produce large flowers of great substance on tall stems ranging from 20 to 24in. high. They are long lasting and the first of the taller bulbous irises to bloom. When planted outdoors in September and October, 3 to 4in. deep and about 5 to 8in. apart, they flower as early as mid-May, going on well into June. Spanish irises bloom at least a fortnight later, while English irises do not flower until late June or July. All are available in separate colours and mixtures.

Ixia. The African Corn Lily is very free flowering, producing on strong, wiry 16 to 18in. stems, graceful heads of delightful blooms, in a wide range of brilliant colours. Flowering outdoors in June and July, each stem boasts six or more flowers of striking beauty, most having a prominent dark centre. The narrow grassy foliage is an added attraction.

Ixiolirion. Of the few species available, *I. pallasii* is the most outstanding and suited to British gardens. It produces lovely large flowers of violet-blue tinged with rose, with a darker coloured band down the centre of each segment.

Lilium. Although many of these are regarded solely as garden plants some are suitable for cutting. Flowering throughout the summer, they include *L. regale*, white with yellow throat and brownish-red on reverse of petals. *L. tenuifolium*, brilliant orange and *L. tigrinum*, red with purple spots. There are many hybrids in separate groups which make admirable cut flowers and these will be detailed in the catalogues of specialists.

Lily of the Valley. This favourite plant is of easy culture if given a soil containing plenty of humus and a partially shaded position. It produces an abundance of scented white bells over many years.

Montbretia. This attractive elegant plant is deservedly popular. Among the best hybrids are Comet, a beautiful rich golden-yellow, each petal being banded crimson; Fiery Cross, on stems of 3ft., bears flowers of brilliant orange with large primrose centre. Hades is vermilion-scarlet with gold throat and small crimson blotch, while Henry VIII is particularly handsome and strong growing, often reaching 3½ft.

Muscari or Grape Hyacinths form little clusters of close-set blue bells on sturdy stems, looking like an up-ended bunch of grapes. They look superb when cut and grouped with the early daffodils, both the white and yellow varieties.

Narcissus flower prolifically. A cluster of a dozen will increase in two or three years to produce as many as fifty to a hundred blooms. Thus when planting, it is advisable to allow 6 to 9in. between the bulbs. As to depth of planting, 5 to 6in. of soil on top of the bulbs is required for their proper development. In light soil plant an inch deeper than in heavy ground. There are varieties growing from 6 to 30in. tall, some with orange or red cups. Daffodils also come in this group since they are technically *narcissus*. Apart from the all-yellow or all-white varieties, some have white petals and yellow or orange trumpets, while a few are shaded pink.

Ornithogalum. In this genus of bulbous plants there are many varieties suitable for cutting. They succeed in well drained soil and are seen at their best planted in groups. Species include: *O. nutans*, producing silvery-grey flowers shaded green on 6 to 9in. stem in May and June; *O. umbellatum*, the Star of Bethlehem, producing starry-white flowers; while *O. pyramidale* has long pointed leaves and in June, pointed white flowers shaded green. *O. arabicum* has on 18in. stems in June and July, creamy-white flowers with shiny black centres.

Puschkinia scilloides. This is useful where miniature flowers are needed for it produces on 4in. stems in March and April, pale blue flowers with a dark stripe. A sandy loam suits this subject which looks well in the front of the border where it can be left undisturbed for years.

Ranunculus. The tuberous species thrive in any good soil so long as the position is unexposed. Planting time is from October to March placing them 2in. deep, claws downwards. The Giant French strain produces semi-double blooms in many colours, while the Double Turban and Turkish strains have large rose-shaped flowers, the mixtures being very long lasting.

Schizostylis. Planted in a sheltered position this is a first-class subject for cutting from late September to November. It makes an ideal pot plant for the cool greenhouse too. *S. coccinea* is crimson-scarlet; Mrs Hegarty, satiny-rose, and Viscountess Byng is flesh-pink.

Scilla. This large family takes in plants of varying size, from those such as *S. bifolia* having bright blue flowers on 4 to 5in. stems in February, to *S. hispanica* and its varieties which grow 12 to 16in. Our native Bluebell, *S. nutans*, also makes a good cut flower if gathered young.

Sparaxis. The Harlequin Flower flourishes in well-drained soil. The best known variety is Scarlet Gem having on 6in. stems, flowers of velvety scarlet with yellow and black centres.

Tulip. This large family takes in flowers having a tremendously wide colour range and flowering over a long period. Apart from the species, the Early Single and Early Double varieties in separate colours, flower from late March until the end of April.

They vary in height from 10 to 16in., and cut when they are fairly young, they are very long lasting. Darwin and Cottage tulips grow 18 to 27 inches high.

CHAPTER 17

HARDY ORCHIDS

WHENEVER ORCHIDS are mentioned, they rightly or wrongly, always conjure up a picture of luxury and many people still imagine that they can only be grown with the help of a high temperature in special glasshouses.

There are of course, a good many which thrive and in fact, almost demand, such great heat, but there are very many more which can be grown with great success where only a small amount of heat can be maintained during the winter. Many cool house orchids are just as exotic looking as some of their famous more delicate relations.

Better still for many gardeners, there is quite a wide selection of hardy orchids which if given the right position, will rival the more highly regarded species and varieties.

There is no doubt that more gardeners will want these hardy kinds once they know of their ease of culture. There are actually a number of the more humble orchids to be found growing wild in woods and the countryside. Few of these are sufficiently showy to give them garden value. In addition, they are rapidly disappearing and most of the places where they can now be found are as far as possible kept secret.

Fortunately, there are good terrestrial species of American, Asian, and continental origin, which will grow well here and particularly in the case of the American and European species, there is no real difficulty in getting them to flower. *Cypripedium calceolus* is the Lady Slipper orchid, once found growing in many of our northern counties, but now almost extinct in the wild. Nurserymen find it always commands a sale, and when planted in sifted loamy leaf mould and partial shade, it normally flowers well.

A site between two large stones is ideal since then the roots will remain cool and the soil will never dry out. The wide leaves are well ribbed and the flowers, on 12in. stems, consist of a yellow lip and lateral petals and a dorsal sepal of a brownish shade, the whole bloom being 2 to 3in. in diameter. Propagation is not easy since the plant dislikes disturbance, but a good way to do this is to scrape away some of the soil around the base of the plant and carefully, without dislodging the whole plant, cut off one or two pieces with roots attached. These can then be potted in the normal way.

The American species *C. parviflorum* or *pubescens*, is very similar and needs identical treatment. It is probably a geographical variant with smaller blooms and long twisted segments on each side of the fat pouch. The loveliest of all the *cypripedium* orchids is *reginae (spectabile)*, the Queen of the Slipper orchids, which has on 15 to 18in. stems, two to four large flowers with a rose-pink lip, white petals and a dorsal sepal making it compare very favourably with many of the exotic indoor species. This too, likes a deep cool, rich soil, and a lightly shaded bed to which manure has been added before planting, is ideal for it.

C. macranthum is an Asiatic species with lovely pale purple flowers. It will thrive in ordinary good garden soil and well decayed leaf mould. *C. speciosum* is somewhat similar but has attractive rose-pink flowers. A little more difficult to establish is *C. californicum*. Given a place where it is happy, it produces six or seven flowers which have a small white lip and brownish petals. It likes a good compost, rich in leaf mould and coarse silver sand, and a position which is sheltered from the east and north east winds is also necessary.

Orchis foliosa is a hardy plant, although it originated from Madeira. It will grow well in pots of deep rich cool soil and seems particularly at home by the waterside. Amid the dark spotted green leaves, it produces racemes of deep purple flowers on 18in. stems. Whenever lifting or handling the fleshy roots, care is necessary so that they are not broken or bruised.

Pleione formosana (pricei) is another fine, more or less hardy, orchid which flourishes in fibrous loam and leaf mould, a valuable addition being fine sphagnum moss. It is also an excellent alpine house plant and produces on 4in. stems, lovely orchid purple and silvery-pink flowers, of which the paler edged petals are prettily fringed. It has several forms including Oriental Splendour distinguished by its purplish-brown bulbs. Moisture during spring and summer are needed, and ideally, drier root conditions when the plant is at rest during the late autumn and winter. It is a good plant for a sheltered position in the rock garden, especially if added protection can be given in the winter.

P. forrestii is another gem. Although introduced to Britain nearly fifty years ago it is still rather rare. It is notable for the fact that it has orange yellow flowers while most of the other species are pink, purple, or crimson.

Bletilla striata (hyacinthina) flourishes in humus-rich soil and will grow outdoors in sheltered nooks while it is also a first-class pot plant. Up to ten large amethyst-purple flowers are produced on each erect, leafy 12 to 15in. stem, in early summer.

Dactylorhiza elata is a hardy orchid from Algeria and splendid for the garden. It likes deep well-enriched, drained soil and a site which never dries out. From the fleshy roots, the sturdy green shoots can often be seen bursting through the soil in late January. These 2ft. leafy stems produce a bold flower head of purple-red.

These are all handsome plants to which the gardener might do well to give more attention, for they are never likely to be over-propagated.

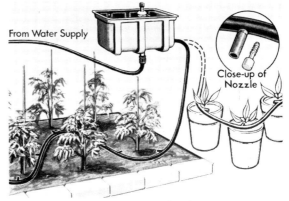

For tomatoes a constant watering device is useful.
Shown is the 'tricklematic' by Humex.

An inexpensive green-
house heater that burns
paraffin.

A greenhouse built from plastic sheeting.

Tasty runner beans, freshly picked, add flavour to your meal. The surplus can be easily frozen and stored for out of season use.

A fine example of round cabbage.

Freshly-picked vegetables, full of flavour – a gourmet's delight.

Gladiolus 'Franks Perfection'.

Crocus 'Striped Beauty'.

Antirrhinum.

Nigella 'Persian Rose'.

A good selection of cacti and succulents.

Helichrysum monstrosum.

Tulipa kaufmanniana.

Galanthus '*Nivalis flore pleno*'.

Wallflowers.

Rhododendron loder 'King George'.

Galanthus elvesii.

A formal wide path. Could be improved by
planting shrubs in containers.

Scilla tubergeniana.

Ornamental Grass.

A shady path bordered by mature trees.

Removing the shuttering for a concrete pond.

Trowelling the cement for a shallow pool.

Primula obconica.

Poppy.

Corner of a cut-flower garden.

Aucuba japonica maculata.

Dahlias provide variety of shape and colour.

Capsicum – **FIPS**.

Colchicum autumnale allium.

Imperial Paeony 'King George VI'.

Scilla silvaner.

Chrysanthemum tricolor.

Euphorbia variegata.

CHAPTER 18

THE GARDEN POOL

WATER PLAYS an important part in nature's landscape and this undoubtedly is why it appeals to garden lovers, offering as it does an opportunity of growing such a variety of interesting and beautiful plants. Then there is the peaceful satisfaction that comes as one is able to observe the varying colour, shape and habit of growth of the plants that can be grown in a pool or stream.

A water-garden whatever its size, can become an outstanding feature in any garden and be just as reliable for providing a display as the herbaceous border or rock garden.

In a few instances it may be possible to make use of a natural stream but in most cases, a water garden will have to be created. Fortunately, construction is within the scope of the average handyman. Traditional construction has been of concrete or brick with the interior surface waterproofed by a rendering of mortar. Now, plastic or rubber linings make construction much easier.

The setting of a formal pool permits interesting variations in garden levels, for the water level can be flush with a terrace, sunk below the garden surface with access by steps, or raised above and made secure by, an ornamental wall. There are taller grasses, bamboos and certain shrubs which will flourish on the north side of a pool and give shelter from cutting north winds.

The size and design of the pool will be largely a matter of choice. One advantage of an irregularly-shaped pool is that there is less possibility of ice exerting pressure and causing leakages, as sometimes happens with straight-sided pools.

If you are making a water-garden do not be too ambitious about size. Digging the hole is the first step and you will need somewhere to put the soil. Fortunately, pools and rock gardens go well together and some of the soil can be used for growing alpine plants; the rest can be used to bank up the sides of the pool.

Aquatic plants need differing depths of water. To provide for this, shelves can be made in the sides of the pool. When excavating the site remember there will be a 4in. layer of concrete on the

G

sides and up to 6in. at the bottom. To make the base firm and extra strong, lay down a layer of large mesh wire netting after 3in. of concrete is in position, then add the remainder. To make the pool waterproof, apply a 1in. thick layer of cement over the whole surface.

If desired, an easy means of draining the pool as necessary can be provided by inserting the top half of a screw top bottle in the cement at or near the base of the pool. If the neck protrudes an inch or so it will be simple to unscrew the top and let out the water. It is also important to provide a soakaway at the base of the pool or from wherever the outlet is made.

Ideally, the cemented pool should be emptied and refilled several times before planting is done. This ensures that any harmful chemical properties from the cement will have vanished, especially if a sealing compound has been used.

During recent years a revolution in pond making has taken place with the introduction of plastic and fibre glass materials. Some of these come in ready shaped glass fibre, bolt-together sections or plastic sheeting; while polythene-lined pools are also much used. Although most of these will last for some years, they cannot be regarded as permanent fixtures. Construction is easy. Simply dig out the hole to the required shape, make sure the base and sides are quite firm, and then lay the plastic sheeting over the hole, weigh down the edges, and fill with water. This will stretch the sheet to the shape of the hole. The surplus material can be trimmed off and an edging placed around the pool.

If fish are to be kept, the pool should be at least 15in. deep. Once installed, established waterfalls and fountains add to the value of a pool and fish thrive in the moving water.

The range of suitable water plants is very wide. Although quite a number of species seem able to live and even flourish without fixing their roots in any soil at all, most do best when they become anchored and can draw nourishment from the compost in which they are planted. Light is important and although nothing can be done about natural streams and ponds, where a pool is being created it is advisable that it should not be entirely overshadowed by trees or buildings.

The best time for planting aquatics is from late April to July, and for water lilies, May and June are the ideal months. Do not put in too many plants. Some species make vigorous growth, overcrowding the water and blotting out smaller and sometimes choicer subjects.

Water lilies and a few other larger subjects which are being placed directly into the pond bed, need a rich rooting mixture and it is best to plant them in baskets, the weight of which will ensure they reach the bottom of the pool. Good loamy soil and old cow manure should be used if possible. It is best not to use poultry or other types of animal manure. The alternative is to mix a 6in. diameter pot full of bone meal in a barrow load of loam.

PAVING AROUND THE POOL

If the area to be paved is on natural undisturbed ground it should be excavated to a depth which allows for the thickness of the paving slabs plus a 3in. in situ concrete base slab and 1in. for bedding mortar for the slabs. However, if the area is on filled ground, or partly filled and partly natural soil, then it is advisable simply to level the surface and bed the paving on sand. The made-up ground is sure to settle, and if a sand bed is used, the slabs can be easily taken up, additional sand added and the slabs relaid. This settlement will probably take place slowly over a period of six to twelve months, so that after about a year, the slabs can be removed, a 3in. thick concrete base slab laid, and the slabs then permanently bedded as described below.

The concrete base slab should be laid with a fall away from the edge of the pool to prevent dirt from being washed into the pool by rain water.

Special precast concrete slabs are obtainable for edging the pool; these are available in various designs, some having a bull-nose edge which provides a handgrip. Nearly all incorporate a special surface to provide a grip for the feet.

There is a wide range of paving slabs varying in colour, texture, size and shape, available for the pool surround. Standard hydraulically-pressed paving flags can also be used.

The slabs should be fully bedded on a nominal 1in. thick layer of mortar, consisting of one part cement, one part lime and six parts plasterers' sand, or one part masonry cement and six parts plasterers' sand. Tap them into place with a stout piece of timber and check for levels with a straight-edge. The joints can be filled later if required. They should be finished $\frac{1}{8}$in. below the level of the slab if the outline of each slab is required to show, and care should be taken to see that mortar does not spread over the surface of the slab. This is particularly important if the slabs are coloured.

Whilst this 'full bed' method of laying paving slabs gives the best results, it requires more care and experience than the 'mortar pad' technique. The latter consists in providing five pads of mortar on the prepared base and then bedding the slab on these, and it is rather easier to obtain an acceptably level surface to the paving than with the previous method. The disadvantages are that any sudden impact load on a slab may cause it to crack, because part of it is hollow underneath (if it is not fully bedded), and that rocking of the slab may occur.

SUBMERGED OXYGENATING AQUATICS

If plants and fish are to flourish in a garden pool or indoor aquarium it is essential for the water to remain pure and clean. To some extent this may be achieved by repeatedly emptying and refilling the pool or container but it is far more satisfactory to plant a sufficient number of submerged oxygenating plants with some of the floating aquatics and to install some water snails.

There is a rich variety of suitable plants from which to choose, both for the outdoor pool and the warm aquarium and there are various reasons why such plants should be grown. First, if the water is not clear any fish present cannot be seen and with cloudy water, the appearance of the pool is unpleasant. Many underwater plants absorb the carbon dioxide from the fish and give out oxygen, while others provide cover for the fish at spawning time.

Healthy submerged plants also prevent algae gaining a proper hold. The minute vegetable organisms which cause algae cannot really thrive without light, so that submerged and floating plants, with the shade they provide, will normally keep the water crystal clear. There is also the point of the waste products from fish and animal life contaminating the water, but much of such debris is absorbed by the plants. Apart from all these considerations, provided the right choice is made, the plants can be of real decorative value.

Fortunately, there is a good range of suitable plants available both for growing in cold water in the open and for warm conditions in aquariums.

In the latter case, planting is done in coarse or aquaria sand, or a thin layer of loam covered with the sand can be used, making this rooting medium about 2in. deep. For a more decorative appearance in fancy bowls or tanks, miniature sand-dunes can be made with small pieces of rock inserted at intervals.

It is unwise to place much material at the bottom since it might lead to crevices in which fish food and other matter can lodge and decompose, possibly leading to trouble.

In outdoor pools submerged plants can be planted into the bed or specially-made pockets of loam. When water is poured directly on to the sand in an aquarium it will obviously become very cloudy and may remain so for some time. To reduce this to the minimum, cover the sand with a piece of muslin or paper and stand a basin of some kind in the centre. If the water is poured into the basin so that as it overflows the aquarium is gradually filled there will be much less trouble with cloudy water. When the tank is three-quarters full, remove the bowl and paper and begin planting.

It is not necessary or desirable for the whole aquarium to be filled with plants but a certain amount of grouping creates a pleasing effect. A flat piece of wood is quite suitable as a planting tool.

Among the most pleasing species of plants available, we can mention only a few of those which have something to recommend them.

Reliable and hardy for outdoors are *Callitriche autumnalis*, with tiny dark green foliage which remains active during the winter months. *C. verna*, the hardy Water Starwort, forms dense tufts of light green foliage rising to the surface during the summer. Make sure it does not become too invasive.

Cardamine rotundifolia, of prostrate habit, has deep green rounded leaves and white flowers. *Ceratophyllum demersum* has fragile branching stems with dense whorls of spiny foliage. It will grow in quite deep water. The little flowers are often followed by small horned fruit. *Eleocharis acicularis*, or Hair Grass, has dense mats of hair-like foliage giving a very graceful effect under water.

Elodea canadensis is a first-class oxygenator which must be kept under control owing to its rampant growth and ability to choke other plants. Do not use it in large ponds or lakes where it might gain such a hold as to strangle choicer subjects. The brittle stems are furnished with oval leaves which are liked by swans and some other water birds.

Fontinalis is the Willow Moss or Water Moss, which indicates the appearance of the plants. First class for ponds, streams and aquaria it is quite happy in running water. It is an excellent oxygenator, and is useful for sheltering the eggs when laid and later the newly-hatched fish.

Potamogeton crispus has prettily crimped foliage which passes from green to a reddish hue in good light. *P. densus* forms clusters of short, light green foliage, while *C. pectinatus* has very fine foliage produced on well branched stems.

Ranunculus aquatilis forms finely cut leaves under the water, while those which appear on the surface have three lobes, which are well shown up by the small white flowers.

Sagittarias, although not really grown as submerged plants, are specially useful for keeping the water in good condition, charging it with oxygen throughout the whole year. There are species suitable for both the outdoor pond and indoor aquarium.

There are literally dozens of other good oxygenating plants but sufficient has been said to show the interesting range available.

FLOATING AQUATICS

Floating aquatics are important, one of their most useful functions being to cast shade, a real need where fish are present, while they check the growth of algae, which can become a nuisance and disfigurement in ponds and pools of all sizes. Floating plants are also of value since they assist aeration by holding bubbles emitted by submerged oxygenators.

The majority do best in shallow water and some like to root in the soil at the margins of pools. There are others which flourish in deep water. None must be allowed to carpet the water entirely for this would exclude the warming influence of the sun and hinder the growth of water lilies and other plants.

The following are a few of the easily obtainable floating plants. *Azolla* the Fairy Floating Moss, assumes delightful red tints in autumn. There are many species, all of which need to be kept under control and it is best not to plant them in small ponds or pools. *A. caroliniana* becomes a beautiful reddish hue in autumn.

Eichhornia speciosa, known as the Water Hyacinth, is most spectacular, its glossy green foliage having curious bladder-like stems. It is not fully hardy and it is advisable to pot up a few roots in autumn and keep them in a frost-proof place. It must be kept in check but the showy pale violet flowers with yellow eye are attractive. The long purplish-black roots attract fish whose eggs can often be seen adhering to the root fibres.

Hydrocharis morsus-ranae, the Frogbit, is a graceful plant with kidney-shaped leaves and three-petalled white flowers. It needs frequent thinning out.

Stratiotes aloides is the Water Soldier, which often remains under the water coming to the surface in midsummer when it produces white flowers.

Ubricularia vulgaris is the Common Bladderwort, which floats just under the surface where the stems, equipped with bladders, trap and absorb small insects. After the yellow flowers fade, the bladders fill with water and the plants sink to the bottom of the pond.

The banks or sides of pools are excellent places for plants that like a moist but not saturated soil. Such plants suggest informality and enhance the appearance of subjects actually in the water.

They include *Aruncus sylvestris*, with much divided foliage and plumes of creamy-white flowers. *Asclepias incarnata*, 2½ to 3ft., has leafy stems and rosy-pink flowers.

Astilbes always look well. They have handsome foliage and plumes of red, pink or silvery-white. *Dodecatheon meadia* has magenta cyclamen-like flowers in spring, while *Gentiana andrewsii* has clusters of rich blue flowers on 2ft. stems in summer. *Gunnera manicata* is a giant rhubarb requiring plenty of room. *Hemerocallis*, the Day Lily in many attractive shades, is particularly good, as are the bog primulas such as *P. pulverulenta, P. beesiana, P. bulleyana* and *P. sikkimensis.*

There are various waterside irises and one, *I. laevigata*, grows 2 to 2½ft. high, the lovely lilac flowers appearing in June. There are both white and pink forms. It is best to plant these in baskets. *I. pseudoacorus* is the yellow Flag Iris. This too, has white and yellow forms, also one with variegated foliage.

I. monspur, I. ochroleuca, I. orientalis and *I. sibirica*, are other first-class species but perhaps the most exciting of all, is the so called Japanese iris, *I. kaempferi*, remarkable for its many named varieties in a wide colour range and for the great size of its flowers which measure up to 6 or 7in. in diameter. They like full sun and should be planted at the water's edge where the crowns are above water level and for preference, where they become reasonably dry when they are dormant.

Lythrum, Marsh Marigold, *Mimulus* and *trilliums* are also pondside plants, which among many others, will be found detailed in nurserymen's catalogues.

There are many ornamental bamboos and grasses which flourish when grown near water and at the same time, provide a natural, informal and yet artistic outline.

Bambusa metake should now be correctly referred to as *Arundinaria japonica*, and this and the other species are quite hardy and will grow well in partial shade. Of the easily grown grasses, *carex, cladium* and *cyperus* are of simple culture. *Elymus glaucus* has upright, silvery leaves on 3ft. stems. *Glyceria aquatica* grows 5 or 6ft. high, so needs plenty of space. There are a number of other species occupying less room.

Miscanthus sinensis with its variegated leaves, and *Phlaris arundinacea picta*, the well-known Ribbon Grass, are both worth including, while *Scirpus cernuus maritimus*, growing 3 to 4ft. high, has triangular stems with brownish flowers on long spikelets.

Ferns also look well near the margins of ponds and streams. They include *Adiantum pedatum*, the hardy Maidenhair fern, *Asplenium blechnum* and *A. dryopteris. Osmunda regalis* is the Royal fern with large fronds. It has several good forms, including one with crested leaves and those which pass to purplish or reddish shades.

Polypodium ferns revel in shady, damp places. The colour of the fronds changes from green to buff and light brown. *Woodwardia augustifolia* is the Chain Fern which likes a really damp position.

Water lilies increase the value and interest whatever the size of the water area. Make sure to choose varieties in keeping with the space available since some species and varieties make a lot of growth and soon crowd out other subjects.

They are best planted in baskets not only because this makes it easy to place them in the pool but it is then simpler to divide the plants as is usually necessary after three years or so. Since water lilies like plenty of phosphates, add bone meal to the compost when making up a planting mixture. The species or varieties grown will largely depend on the depth of the water. The small growing sorts need at least 6in., the large growers 2 to 3ft. May and June are the best months to plant.

The colour range of *nymphaeas* is good and includes: white – *N. alba, N. candida*; Pink *N. laydekeri, N. marliacea, N. somptuosa*; Red – *N. ellisiana, N. frobelii, N. gloriosa, N. ‘*William

Falconer '; Yellow – *N. moorei, N. odorata sulphurea* and Sunrise. *N. aurora* opens yellow then changes to orange and red.

While trees and shrubs really should not overhang the pond or stream, they do add to the attractiveness of the water surrounds. Among suitable subjects are the following. *Alnus incisa* a bush with well cut foliage. *Alnus cordifolia* makes a fine tree with long catkins during winter. Many poplars are suitable, including *P. balsamifera* with scented foliage, and *P. tremula* with 'perpetual motion' leaves. *Taxodium distichum* is the Swamp Cypress, a handsome deciduous conifer.

Other subjects one can depend on include: *Acer rubrum*, the Red Maple; *Betula nana*, a low growing birch; *Cornus alba*; *Hippophae rhamnoides* the Sea Buckthorn; Willows and Vacciniums.

The pleasure in having made a pool and planted it with suitable subjects is sometimes dampened by the sight of the water becoming murky and discoloured. In established ponds water remains clear for years. On close inspection one can often find long, thick stringlike growths clinging to the plants or the sides of the pond. These are forms of algae which appear quite naturally.

They grow if water is exposed to light as will be seen if a container of water is allowed to stand in a sunny window for some days. Since a sheltered site, exposed to sunshine is ideal for a pond or pool, and the plants are set in fertile soil, these are the right conditions for the spread of algae, especially when combined with leaves, dust and unconsumed fish food.

The trouble is less likely to occur when lilies are planted in baskets or on the pond base and the surface soil is dressed with a layer of fine clear shingle which prevents the fish stirring up mud. Filling the pond gradually helps in not disturbing the soil too sharply.

An additional way of stopping algae from developing is to introduce plenty of the submerged oxygenating plants previously mentioned. These compete with algae for light and food. They spread rapidly, oxygenating the water as well as providing shelter for fish eggs. Undoubtedly they are the key to water clarity. They make hardly any roots although it is possible to induce plants to sink to the bottom by placing a light weight round some of the growths.

Submerged oxygenating plants absorb mineral salts through stems and leaves. To keep the water really clear, plant them at the rate of ten to twelve for every 24sq. ft. of water surface.

Sometimes what appear to be lumps of jelly are seen on the undersides of water lilies and other large leaved plants. These are the egg clusters of water snails and are not harmful.

CHAPTER 19

THE VEGETABLE GARDEN

WHILE IT may be true that as we grow older our taste buds are less lively, there is little doubt that many of the vegetables eaten today lack flavour. This may be due to the variety being grown for undoubtedly some varieties are much tastier than others.

It does not follow that a vegetable variety introduced with great publicity is better flavoured than an old form, in fact, one notable point about newly-produced varieties is that very little is said about flavour but much about size.

By careful selection made as the result of one's own experience and after perusal of specialists' catalogues it is possible to concentrate on fine flavoured subjects. The items now indicated in alphabetical order are among the best and have no difficult cultural requirements.

ARTICHOKES

There are at at least three very different plants known as artichokes which are of value as vegetables. First is the Globe artichoke, of which the bud can be eaten. The flower is spectacular and the foliage ideal for floral arrangements. Evergreen, it provides good ground cover.

Of upright habit *Cynara scolymus*, its correct name, grows 4 to 6ft. high, the well cut leaves, 2 to 3ft. long, being greyish-green with white down on the undersides. The purple flowers produced in autumn are surrounded by an involucre consisting of fleshy scales which are the edible portion of the plant. The flower heads should be cut with a few inches of stem when young and tender, before the scales are fully developed.

Globe artichokes are most suitable for growing in warmer districts where the crowns can be covered during severe weather. Move the ground deeply during the early winter, working in plenty of dung or good compost, and plant the roots from March to May. This will give a succession of heads from June to early October, especially if strong suckers are used.

Place the roots firmly 2½ft. apart with 4ft. between rows. In good soil, Globe artichokes remain productive for five or six years. An annual winter dressing of decayed farmyard manure encourages good quality heads. Gather the heads as soon as they are ready. If they are not to be used immediately the stems can be placed in water where they keep fresh for some days. After the largest central king heads have been cut, side buds will develop.

Varieties include: Green Globe and Purple Globe, the former being hardier and having fewer prickles. Gros Vert de Laon is a good well-flavoured French variety.

Jerusalem artichokes. Probably the most popular of artichokes, the word Jerusalem is a corruption of an Italian word girasole used for *Helianthus tuberosus*, the Sunflower. The name artichoke was given to denote the similarity in the flavour of this root to the Globe artichoke scales.

These hardy perennial plants can be used as windbreaks; as a division or screen in the garden, or for protecting tender crops, since they grow 6 to 7ft. high. They grow best in deeply-dug enriched medium to light soil, fish manure being most beneficial. On heavy ground slugs may become a nuisance. Weathered ashes or silver sand used as surface dressing keeps pests away.

Place tubers about the size of a pullet's egg 6in. deep and 10 to 12in. apart, covering them lightly, and working in fish manure or other organic fertiliser. Allow 3ft. between rows. Once growth starts, draw up soil towards the plants. In exposed windy places, a stake at the end of each row connected with two or three strands of wire or thin string will keep the plants upright.

If the plants show signs of flowering remove the buds so that the strength of the plants is devoted to the production of tubers. Towards the end of October cut off top growth within 12in. of the soil. The tubers are hardy and can be left in the ground and lifted as required. Freshly dug they are better flavoured than when stored although it is possible to store the tubers in boxes of sand or soil or to place them in clamps.

Varieties: New White is of excellent flavour and better than the purple skinned sort. Fuseau has smooth tubers which are easier to deal with in the kitchen. They lack the smoky flavour of the other varieties, and are particularly good eaten when young. Boil the tubers in their skins. Do not peel until ready to serve.

Chinese artichokes. The Chinese artichoke is not an artichoke at all but *Stachys tuberifera*. It is probable that the common name was given because the flavour resembles that of the true artichoke.

The spirally twisted tubers vary in length from 1 to 3in. At their widest part they are about an inch thick.

They flourish on a well-cultivated light soil where the situation is sunny. On poor ground work in compost or organic fertiliser before planting in March and April. Place the tubers 4in. deep and 9in. apart with 15 to 18in. between rows.

The tubers mature from November onwards and should be dug as required. Use them as soon as lifted, never allow them to remain in the light or they will become discoloured. If stored under cover for any length of time they may grow again and become flavourless and useless.

Cardoon. A near relative of the Globe artichoke, this handsome plant, which botanically is *Cynara cardunculus*, has silvery fern-like foliage. It is grown for its blanched stalks which are not unlike the chards produced by Globe artichokes. These are used in the same way as celery, both subjects requiring similar culture.

Cardoons like rich moist soil and succeed in trenches about 12in. deep and 8in. wide where there is manure or decayed compost at the bottom. Plants can be raised from seed sown from March onwards keeping the roots moist throughout the summer. Occasional applications of liquid manure will encourage tender growth.

From mid-September the plants will be ready for blanching. For this, tie all the leaves together and then earth up as for celery, or place corrugated tubes over the plants. Alternatively, bracken or straw can be used for a covering. The process takes six to eight weeks, but make sure the stems are dry before commencing to blanch.

There are two main sorts. The French cardoon often listed as Tours, has long stems with prickles which make it difficult to work among the plants. The Spanish cardoon is spineless but the flavour is not so good and the plants are apt to run to seed.

ASPARAGUS

Far too many gardeners are of the opinion that the growing of asparagus involves some difficult procedure. This crop is often regarded as a luxury vegetable intended for those who have special facilities available. This is not so, for although care is needed, an asparagus bed is fairly easy to make and little attention is required in maintaining it in productive condition.

The first essential in growing this vegetable is bulky manure of some kind. Where farmyard manure is not available, a good organic substitute should be used. This should be placed 18in. below the surface. If the land is on the heavy side the addition of silver sand or burnt earth will be beneficial. A lime content of approximately ph 7 is best.

The exact method of planting is a matter of local convenience. Single independent rows 4ft. apart with crowns 15in. apart are ideal but where space is limited the rows can be closer. Place the crowns 4 to 5in. deep. The roots spread out well and need a lot of space. The planting season is rather brief and should be completed between 21 March and 10 April.

Never let the roots dry out when they are being planted. Crowns from one to three years old are available and the older crowns will naturally come into full cutting earlier than the young plants. Young crowns will usually settle down better. It is unwise to take a crop the first year. It is best to allow the plants to become established. Since a well-planned bed can be expected to remain in production for at least ten years, it is important that a good strain is secured.

Asparagus can be forced in frames or boxes without difficulty. Always allow some ' fern ' to develop. This is needed to build up the crowns for the following year. When it is quite brown it can be cut and removed from the beds with any seeds that may have formed. One is sometimes advised to buy male crowns, but these are not generally offered as such by suppliers.

Good varieties are: Argenteuil, and Connover's Colossal.

CALABRESE

This is the green sprouting broccoli, an excellent vegetable for summer and autumn use. Culture is the same as for other types of broccoli. Sow the seed in spring and set out the plants in June. Calabrese differs from other broccoli in that it first produces a good sized, loose green central head of 6in. or more in diameter. This is cut out and cooked in the usual way but it is the shoots or sprouts which then develop that are the great delicacy. These are cut when 4 to 6in. long. The leaves can be removed and the stems lightly peeled before the sprouts are steamed or boiled. Calabrese crops very heavily, partly due to the fact that the sprouts are produced from September onwards when weather conditions are really good.

CAPSICUM

Capsicum frutescens, (annuum) often known as the Sweet Pepper, is best grown in the greenhouse or frame unless the summer is really hot. It flourishes in humus-rich compost.

The simplest way is to grow them in large pots. Then in really good weather they can be moved into the garden, and put under glass again if and when it becomes cooler. Sow the seed in March in a temperature of 60° F (16° C) and move the plants to their final positions in the greenhouse, border, frame, cloche or pots in mid-May. The plants usually branch naturally. If they do not, pinch out the growing point to encourage side shoots to develop.

Keep them well ventilated and watered, and once the fruit begins to swell, give a few liquid feeds at ten-day intervals.

Pick the peppers when they are a good size and a deep shining green colour, or in the case of the red strains when they are nicely coloured.

Capsicums vary in length from 4 to 5in. although the bull-nosed types are usually only 2 to 3in. long.

The Chilli peppers, *C. longum*, being very hot tasting, are used chiefly for flavouring and pickles.

CELERIAC

This is a form of celery and although the foliage may be used to flavour soups and stews, this crop is grown for its roundish large swollen stems. These look rather like swedes although they have the flavour of celery.

Seed is sown early in the year in the warm greenhouse, the seedlings being planted out of doors in good fertile land in June. Plentiful supplies of moisture must always be available both to prevent the plants from bolting and to encourage the bulbing of the stems. It is helpful if the soil contains plenty of humus matter. As a further aid to good results a top dressing of compost or peat will prevent the soil from drying out. All side shoots must be removed as soon as seen. The crop should be lifted in October and the foliage removed before the swollen stems are stored in boxes of damp sand or peat.

Giant Prague and Early Erfurt are most reliable.

CELERY

Both pink and white celery is a much valued crop and most gardeners grow it successfully provided the trenches are well-enriched and properly prepared. Few gardeners attempt to grow self-blanching celery although it is not difficult to cultivate. Soil is important for this crop demands ground rich in organic matter.

Apart from open ground culture, self-blanching celery can be grown where a modified form of French gardening is practised. On suitable well-manured soils, hot bed frames can be used effectively for this crop which can follow early carrots. Sow seed in early March. February sowings are liable to run to seed.

There are white and cream varieties, the Golden Self-Blanching being most popular. The very fine seed needs to be sown thinly. Pots or boxes should be watered the day before pricking out the seedlings into firm beds 2 to 3in. apart each way. Later, move them to the open ground or frames, allowing 9in. each way. It is usually about the first week in July before the plants can be put into their final quarters.

Basic cultural operations required for the remainder of the season are hoeing, weeding, watering, blight control and sometimes, help with blanching.

The close planting suggested normally leads to blanched stems but some improvement can be obtained by placing clean dry straw between the rows ten days before the crop is gathered. The crop must be harvested prior to severe frosts. Self-blanching celery usually matures from September onwards, before ordinary celery is ready for use.

Green Celery. This is a fairly recent introduction from the United States. Although the head is green, the flavour is mild and much liked by some people. The plants are raised in exactly the same way as the normal white celery which is blanched. Green celery matures in September and should be harvested before the frosts come.

CHICORY

Many people think of chicory as something for mixing with coffee. It is the Magdeburg Chicory which, after drying, roasting and grinding, is used for this purpose. For providing a delicious salad in winter and spring, however, the Brussels Witloof Chicory should be grown. This becomes available when lettuce and endive are usually scarce and expensive. It can also be eaten, like celery, with cheese, and can be stewed and served with melted butter in the same way as seakale.

Sow the seed from late May onwards making the rows 18in. apart and thinning the seedlings so that there is a foot between them. Forcing begins in October when the roots are lifted from the open ground.

Although the roots can be forwarded in sheds or cool or cold greenhouses, forcing is better, but too much warmth leads to unwanted soft, drawn heads.

Chicory is ready for cutting when the tops, known as chicons, start to show through the soil. They should be kept out of the light, and this also applies after the heads are cut, otherwise they turn green and become bitter and useless.

Chicory

A forced chicon.

Chicory roots set upright in the bottom box in soil and a bottomless box placed over it. This second box will contain the dry soil to give a 7 inch cover to the roots.

CORN SALAD

The proper name of this subject is *Valerianella olitoria*, while it is sometimes referred to as Lamb's Lettuce, and there are now several improved cultivated forms.

Corn Salad is hardy, easily grown, and a useful substitute for lettuce during the winter. In appearance it is not unlike the Forget-me-Not without the blue flowers. It makes an excellent cloche crop and is eaten either raw or cooked. Sowings can be

H

made at intervals from the end of July until late September, thus providing supplies from autumn until spring.

Sow the seed thinly in drills ¾in. deep and a foot apart. Since germination is sometimes erratic, sowing is best done in showery weather when the soil is moist. The drills should not be left open before the seed is sown, otherwise they will dry out. Thin out the young plants so that they stand about 6in. apart.

COURGETTES

Seed is sown and the plants are grown just like the ordinary bush type of vegetable marrow, of which in fact, they are a variety.

Zucchini and *Courgette* are two of the best and most popular. The plants must be grown in fertile soil and kept well-watered in dry weather for only thus will the full flavour develop. Courgettes must be cut while small, anything between 3 and 5in. long. The more you cut the greater will be the total crop. When only 3 or 4in. long they can be cooked whole and unpeeled. Slightly larger specimens should be sliced. Courgettes may be regarded as a luxury vegetable in the same category as asparagus but they are easier to grow and more productive. Cooked in butter they are a real delicacy. If you have only eaten supplies from the shop, you have not tasted the deliciousness of freshly-gathered courgettes.

COUVE TRONCHUDA

Sometimes known as the Portugal Cabbage, this little-known vegetable has been in cultivation for 150 years. It is unsuitable for small gardens since it needs a spacing of at least 2½ft. each way.

It can be described as a kind of cabbage of which the mid-rib is larger than the leaves, for with well-grown plants, the mid-ribs are thick, white and tender. Cooked like seakale, they are delicious. The green parts and the centre of the plants can be used as ordinary cabbages but must be carefully cooked, otherwise they become coarse and stringy.

The plants are raised in the same way as cabbages and should be grown on fairly rich, moisture-holding soil in unexposed positions.

CUCUMBERS

Good greenhouse or frame-grown cucumbers cannot be bettered for flavour, but they do require rather more care in their cultivation than many other types of vegetable crops.

Preparation of the growing position is important and there is nothing better than good clean straw, horse manure and turfy loam which has not been stacked too long (such loam will have lost a good deal of its fibre and will be inclined to dry out frequently). Tests have shown that two parts of loam to one of strawy manure are about right. Bone meal and hoof and horn can be mixed either with the loam or when it has been mixed with the manure, while a 60 size potful of chalk to each barrow load of loam is beneficial.

Sow seed in the ordinary 14 by 9in. seed boxes or in pans, filling them with compost made from good clear fibrous loam and well rotted horse manure, to within ½in. of the top, using a fairly open but not too fine soil mixture. Cover the boxes with glass and paper and place them on the staging in a temperature of at least 65° F (18° C). Rapid germination is required and this usually takes place within three days. The glass is then removed. From this time on a moist atmosphere is needed.

When placing the plants in their fruiting positions make the holes in the bed large enough to drop in the ball of soil and roots and carefully firm the soil around the little stems. Allow at least 2ft. each way between the plants. A stake should be placed near each plant so that the growth can run up on to the horizontal wires.

Keep on training the growths up the wires and also regularly take out the growing points. The main stem is allowed to grow to the top of the wire and is then stopped. Side shoots will develop which will need stopping at the second joint and then tying in. Sub-laterals will also require stopping at the first joint and this process continues while the plants remain fully active.

Cutting must be done regularly once the plants come into bearing. January sowings do not usually mature until late March, but from spring sowings cutting should be possible in about six or seven weeks.

Reliable varieties include: Telegraph, Conqueror and Green Spot, an F.1 hybrid similar to Butcher's Disease Resisting. Victory is an F.1. hybrid producing only female flowers and fruit which is not bitter.

Some years ago as a result of research and patient study of trials, the so-called cordon cucumber was developed at F. G. Read's nurseries near Norwich. This cucumber is exceptional for its sustained vigour and first-class fruits which are often produced within six weeks of seed sowing. Individual fruits are straight and of attractive appearance. The weight and quality of the crop depends upon the skill of the individual grower and the usual culture being followed. Fruits begin to appear in clusters of five to seven at the base of the rough leaves and provided the plants are in good condition all should be allowed to mature as they quickly become ready for cutting.

The ridge or outdoor cucumber should be grown in fairly rich soil but fresh manure should be avoided. Plant on little mounds with well-rotted manure placed at the bottom. Seed is sown in the warm greenhouse or frame in April and once the first leaves have developed pot them singly into 2½in. pots where they remain until planted outdoors at the end of May. Plenty of moisture is needed during dry weather. Best results come from Stockwood Ridge and Greenline.

ENDIVE

Much more popular on the continent than in Britain, endive is an excellent salad plant for use during the winter months. So long as the leaves are blanched they are very palatable, otherwise they have a bitter taste.

For best results and winter production, the seed should be sown at intervals from mid-June until the first half of August. Make up a good seed bed and sow the seed thinly in drills ½in. deep and 6in. apart. Prick out the seedlings when they are easy to handle and later plant them 12in. apart in positions where they can be covered with the lights.

Blanching can usually be started between three and four months from the time of sowing, and if the lights are well coated with whitewash on the underside of the glass, it will ensure the necessary darkness. Straw or sacking laid on the lights will intensify this darkness and give protection during very cold weather.

The period required for blanching varies from ten days to three or four weeks. Make sure that the plants are dry before covering them with darkened lights and it is helpful if the leaves are given a light tie.

Of the varieties available, Ruffec and Meaux are both good but the Batavian endive is hardier and therefore more suitable for winter work.

GARLIC

For long reckoned to have health promoting qualities, garlic is valued by many cooks and gourmets because among its uses, it increases the good flavour of other ingredients in salads and sandwich fillings.

Although quite hardy, the plants grow best in a fairly sheltered position and a light dryish soil. Ground manured for a previous crop is ideal, especially if weathered soot and wood ashes are raked in.

Garlic forms a number of bulblets or cloves, a well-developed specimen consisting of up to two dozen. Planting should be done in March, although in really warm districts where the soil is light, November plantings give good results. Space the cloves 9in. apart with rows a foot asunder. Cover them with 2in. of soil.

Garlic

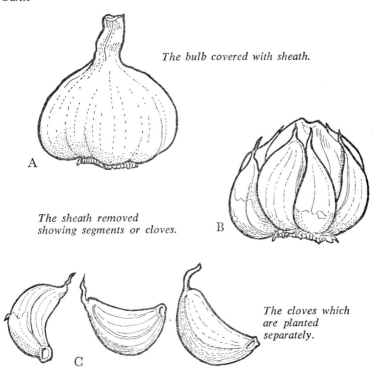

The bulb covered with sheath.

A

The sheath removed showing segments or cloves.

B

C

The cloves which are planted separately.

By mid-July the leaves will have withered, a sign that the cloves are ready for lifting and drying. Properly dried and stored, garlic keeps well for many months.

GHERKINS

Grown for pickling, the aim should be to produce succulent fruits up to 3in. long. This means they must be gathered before they become larger and coarse. General culture is the same as for ridge cucumbers.

It is best to sow the seeds in their growing positions. Do this early in June in prepared sites, enriched with bulky manure or compost to encourage a good root system. Plant the seeds an inch deep and if two are sown at each station, the weakest seedling can be pulled out later.

Varieties include Boston Pickling, Small Paris and Model.

GOOD KING HENRY

Often known as Mercury this vegetable is of easy cultivation. Seeds can be sown in drills for thinning out later but are best sown where the plants are to grow, from mid-April onwards, making the rows 2ft. apart and thinning the plants so there is 18in. between them. It is also possible to divide older plants but make sure each division has a strong separate crown.

On good land, the plants produce from April to June, numerous shoots which should be gathered while young and cooked like asparagus. Left to grow old, the skin toughens and needs to be removed before cooking.

GOURDS – See Pumpkins.

KOHL RABI

Sometimes known as the cabbage-turnip, Kohl Rabi has been in cultivation for many years. Although fairly widely used on the Continent it is not much grown in this country.

This vegetable should be used when the roots are the size of a cricket ball. It has a distinct nutty flavour provided the roots are used before they become large.

The edible portion is the knob-like growth which appears just above ground level. This, however, should not be cooked in the same way as turnips but is best peeled and sliced before being boiled or steamed. If roots are used while they are small it is not essential to peel them. The steamed roots can be fried and are very tasty.

Sow in March and April either broadcast or in drills 15in. apart. The roots can be used from August onwards.

ONIONS

While chives and garlic are the best known of the other types of onions, there are other kinds worthy of cultivation including Japanese Bunching. This is a perennial plant which retains its foliage throughout the winter. The leaves are excellent for flavouring while their silvery-white stems or scallions are valuable in the salad bowl. Easy to grow, this plant can be raised from seed sown in the spring, the young plants first being thinned and later moved to their permanent positions in the autumn.

Potato or underground onion. Grown chiefly in Ireland this is of value where it is difficult to produce good onions from seed. They like well-drained soil and an open but unexposed position. Well-rotted manure will help to retain the moisture the plants like. Plant in March or early April setting them 8 or 9in. apart with a foot between the rows.

Towards the end of August the soil should be carefully scraped away from the bulbs to encourage the ripening process. Each bulb produces a number of offsets some of which can be used for planting the next spring.

Tree Onion. Sometimes known as the Egyptian onion, this is a hardy perennial of Canadian origin. It is specially useful where onion fly is troublesome. It grows about 4ft. high and in addition to the bulbs it forms in the ground, clusters of onions develop at the top of the stem. Valuable for pickling and flavouring, they are rather hot to taste. Sets or bulbs can be planted in spring or autumn, placing them 10 to 12in. apart and 1in. deep.

Welsh Onion. This is not Welsh at all but comes from Siberia! Very hardy, it does not form real bulbs but produces many white scallions or chibols which are used as spring onions. Sometimes known as Japanese leeks they like a well-drained position. Plants can be raised from seed sown in March. Thin out the seedlings in the ordinary way, spacing them 9 to 12in. apart. Dig up the entire plants and separate the stems for use.

PEAS

There are a number of unusual varieties, which although not always easy to obtain, are well worth growing because of their distinct and pleasing flavour. These include the following:

Asparagus Peas. This is an ornamental plant as well as one producing edible pods. It is because of the flavour of the pods, which should be picked while small and cooked whole, that asparagus comes into the name. Botanically the plant is *Lotus tetragolobus purpureus* having brownish-red flowers, the pods being triangular shaped.

It is best to sow seed in warmth in April, hardening off the seedlings for planting outdoors in late May when seed can also be sown in the open. A sunny position and light soil suits this crop.

Carlin Pea. This is grown chiefly in the north of England and used especially on Mid-Lent Sunday, once widely known as Carlin Sunday. Cultivation is the same as for other types, the dark coloured seed being sown in April.

The plants grow 6 or 7ft. high and need staking. They are rarely attacked by disease or pests, and birds and mice leave them alone. The dried seeds are soaked well for some hours before being cooked. Sprinkled with sugar and rum the flavour is superb.

The Purple Podded Pea. This has flowers and pods of a purplish shade. It grows 4 to 5ft. high and needs the normal cultivation for peas. Of excellent flavour the pods can be used fresh or dried for winter eating.

Petit Pois. One of the most delicious vegetables. Sow seed in April allowing 3ft. between rows, and providing 3 to 4ft. supports. Gather the pods once they are filled. If they are steamed whole without delay, they will readily fall from the pods, with their wonderful sugary flavour.

Sugar Pea. Gathered when young these are a real delicacy. The entire pods are eaten after being topped and tailed. Pick the pods when the peas are beginning to swell. Several strains are available, the Mange Tout so popular in France, growing 4 to 5ft. while Sweet Pod is another heavy cropper of pods of sweet flavour. Sweetgreen is a dwarf variety no more than 18in. high.

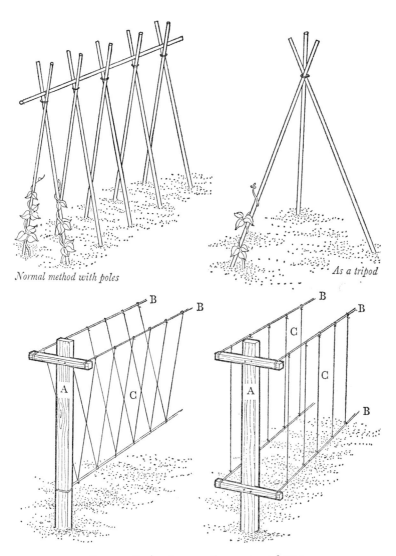

Normal method with poles

As a tripod

Four methods of supporting peas or beans.

POTATOES TO GROW FOR FLAVOUR

Golden Wonder. One of the best flavoured of all varieties. A white-fleshed floury kidney main crop, but not a very reliable cropper.

Duke of York, has yellow flesh of good flavour. Its small haulm makes it valuable for growing in frames or under cloches. Good for frying and baking.

Epicure. A reliable early variety, the round, white fleshed tubers being of fine flavour. Its deep eyes lessen its popularity.

Home Guard. One of the earliest varieties which scrapes easily. The white waxy flesh is of fine flavour which is at its best during the first few months after lifting. Good for chipping.

Ulster Premier. White fleshed, rarely discolours after cooking. Is best used within three or four months of lifting.

Record. This is one of the best flavoured of all potatoes being particularly useful for boiling and frying. A good keeper, it is one of the varieties widely grown for potato crisps.

Craig's Royal. White-fleshed kidney-shaped main crop. Does not boil to mash.

King Edward VII. A kidney of first-rate appearance, quality, and flavour. Does best where the soil is on the rich side.

Pentland Crown. Its flavour is at its finest from early January onwards. Resistant to scab, it stands up to drought.

Maris Page. A second early blight-resistant variety. Fries and bakes well.

Orion. Not very easy to obtain, this is a main crop with pale lemon flesh; first class for mashing.

French salad potatoes. These have rather long, rounded tubers and yellow flesh, are of excellent flavour and invaluable for salads and frying. Particularly reliable varieties are Pink Fir Apple and Aura.

SALSIFY

This is a biennial plant, often known as the Vegetable Oyster because of its flavour. Not at all widely grown in this country it is much in use as a winter vegetable in France and Italy. It likes a deep moisture retentive soil on the light side, preferably one enriched with decayed manure or compost the previous season.

Sow seed in mid-April in drills an inch deep and 12in. apart, and thin the seedlings to 6 or 7in. apart. The roots are ready for use from October onwards and may be lifted as required, and treated like parsnips. Take care not to damage them or they will bleed and lose their nutty flavour.

If some plants are left in the ground during the winter young top growth can be cut and cooked in spring when they have an asparagus-like flavour. The cream-coloured roots should be 6 to 9in. long and 2in. thick. They can be steamed or boiled in their skins, which are rubbed off, before being served with white sauce. The variety usually available is known as Sandwich Island Mammoth.

SCORZONERA

Very similar to salsify, this is preferred by many because of its flavour and its help in various forms of indigestion. Fertile soil free from clods or stones ensures straight roots. Sow seed from April onwards in drills 1in. deep and 15in. apart. Thin the seedlings early, leaving strong plants 6in. apart. The plants are perfectly hardy and while roots can be stored in boxes of sand, it is better to lift as required and cook without delay.

Boil or steam the roots before peeling. The black skin is not easy to remove, the best way being to rub them in a cloth while the roots are hot.

If they are left in the ground for a second year the plants often produce flowers. In ancient cookery books, we read that if flower buds are gathered, washed and dried, they can be cooked in butter until they are brown and then mixed with eggs for making omelets.

SWEET CORN

During the last thirty years, sweet corn has become widely known in this country, although it is unsuited to high altitudes and places exposed to sea winds. For an early crop and where small quantities are involved, seed can be sown in Jiffy Pots or in large 60 size pots from the second week in April onwards, for planting outdoors during early June. Do not sow before or the roots may become pot-bound. Seed can also be sown in cold frames where the plants can be left to mature, or cloches are useful for covering direct open ground sowings.

For uncovered sowings, from the third week in May onwards, 2in. deep furrows are drawn out in fine soil. Two seeds are dropped in at 15in. intervals or singly 9 to 12in. apart. Space the rows 21 to 24in. apart, the greater distance for the latest sorts.

Sweet corn is wind and insect pollenated and carries male and female flowers on the same plant. The plants are best grown in blocks of three or four short rows so that pollen from the tassels at the top of the plants falls on to the ' silks ' which hang from the embryo cobs.

Proper harvesting influences yield and it is essential to gather only fully-developed cobs. Picking begins about the third week in August. If a creamy solution springs from the grains when pressed with the thumbnail they are definitely ripe. When the silks have changed to a brownish-black colour and are shrivelling, the cob is at the eating stage.

Once the cobs are twisted off the plants, the grains start to become starchy, which is why freshly-gathered cobs are so much nicer than those stored a long time before they are eaten.

Varieties: Golden Bantam, early sweet and tender. Prima, fourteen days earlier than Golden Bantam, and Kelvedon Glory, an F.1 hybrid of first-class table quality.

WATERCRESS

It has long been known that watercress is ' good for you ' and eaten raw regularly, its health-giving properties will soon prove beneficial. The value of watercress is that it is available over a very long period, being particularly useful at times when other salad ingredients are scarce. It has a high mineral content, exceeding that of lettuce and salad onions, while its vitamins C and B content are also high.

Many people say they do not like watercress, and perhaps the reason is that so often it is only seen in greengrocers' shops as a bundle of discoloured, wizened leafy stalks.

Henslow in his book *The Use of British Plants* says ' the latin name is derived from nasus – the nose, and tortus – twisted, from the pungent sensation. It was familiar to the ancient Greeks as Kardamon being used for salads and for its medicinal value '. In Pliny's time it was recorded as ' efficacious for brain disorders and insanity ', the Greek name meaning ' head subduer '. Its nutritive value depends upon the aromatic oil and mineral ingredients in which it exceeds all other salad plants.

Various sorts of watercress are in cultivation, all derived from the wild and hybrid types. Most bear little resemblance to the original species. They are divided into two main groups, the green, which is available in summer, and the brown or winter strains which are most in demand.

The green form produces long shoots which do not always branch well. This as I have found can be a drawback if the growing area is limited. In addition, they only seem to flourish where the temperature of the water rises during spring and summer. This does have the advantage of making them suitable for growing in streams and other shallow water.

The origin of brown watercress is obscure, it may have come as a sport or mutation. If it has, the mutations must have been fairly frequent since they have appeared at different times in various parts of the country. The depth of colour of the brown strains seems to depend on both climatic conditions and water temperature. The poorer the conditions the deeper the brown tinge, and prolonged exposure to cold winds deepens the colour even more.

Watercress can be propagated from seed or cuttings. In the case of the former, sowing can be done from mid-June to mid-August on an almost dry seed bed. Sprinkle seed thinly on the surface, then admit a trickle of water to encourage germination which normally occurs within a week. A tap root is soon formed. The seed bed should then be pressed down to consolidate the soil and to encourage a mat of roots to form.

While running water is ideal for growing watercress, a crop can be secured without it. This can be done by selecting a shaded position where the soil contains plenty of organic matter, making it moisture retentive. If the site is naturally on the dry side trenches up to 8in. deep can be made and filled with vegetable compost, covering this with 2in. of soil so that the finished trench is a little below the surrounding soil.

Watercress plants are easy to propagate from cuttings using sturdy shoots. Do this in May and June for autumn and winter cropping, and in September and October for spring and summer cutting.

Landcress, sometimes known as American cress, can be grown in the open ground preferably in cool, partially-shaded beds. The top soil should contain plenty of organic matter to retain moisture.

CHAPTER 20

THE HERB GARDEN

THE HERB garden can be both a fascinating and decorative feature in any garden. There is no standard size; it can be anything from a yard square patch near the kitchen door to an elaborate creation of several hundred square feet. Shape is not important, in fact, many informal irregularly shaped borders have been cultivated for centuries. In the larger gardens winding paths and little nooks add to the attractiveness of the display. Alternatively a well-planned formal herb garden can become a central feature especially since so many herbs are evergreen.

Apart from being grouped in separate gardens, subjects such as rosemary and lavender can be used for hedges and give a sense of maturity. The old English lavender is inclined to become leggy unless cut back annually. For low hedges, Dwarf Munstead is ideal, while there is a compact pink flowering lavender.

Rosemary is also valuable for hedging particularly where something of a spiky nature is required. The showy blue flowers are produced in May. For lower growing hedges or dividing lines, southernwood and santolina are useful.

Knot Gardens were once fashionable and, well kept, they give an air of distinction to any garden. They may be made in various forms, one of the easiest being the shape of a wheel, the spokes being made of close growing herbs such as hyssop, rue and thyme, the spaces in between being planted with carpeting subjects. It is also possible to make elaborately-shaped knot gardens in the form of a crown, a rose or even a castle.

Herb seats are sometimes made. These are cut out of a bank and creeping subjects such as chamomile, thyme and *Mentha requieni* used for a ' covering '.

Not every garden has room for a separate herb section and often one can only grow a small number. Among the vast range of plants referred to as ' herbs ' the following are particularly valuable. Most of them have a number of uses, some having been employed for medicinal purposes as well as used for flavouring soups, stews, salads and stuffings; others are included for their perfume and for improving punches and ' teas '.

Herbs are steeped in history. Certain species were once held to ward off evil powers and were used in potions, and for curing obscure complaints.

ALECOST

Valued by cooks, the leaves are chopped finely for using in stuffings and soups and when dried are useful in pot pourris.

ANGELICA

This flourishes in light soil where there is slight shade. Growing 3 to 6ft. high, the leaves are daintily sculptured with white flowers appearing in May and June. The stem may be stewed with rhubarb while the roots and dried leaves are used medicinally. The stems are often candied and most cooks will know the process involved.

ANISE

An annual growing 2ft. high, seed can be sown in April and May. The aromatic seeds produced in late summer are used for flavouring or in cakes and liqueurs, while they have some value in clearing coughs and chest troubles.

BALM LEMON

Sometimes found growing wild, this hardy perennial reaches a height of 3 to 4ft. and has nettle-like foliage and small whitish flowers. The leaves are particularly useful when dried and added to herb mixtures while they add zest to salads. Excellent bee plants, they were once used to soothe nervous disorders. Variegated Balm has yellow flecked leaves.

BASIL

Bush basil is usually grown as an annual, Sweet basil being the perennial. They are strongly-flavoured aromatic herbs invaluable for flavouring stews and soups, whilst the fresh leaves are pleasant additions to salads. Early sowings can be made under glass; otherwise seed can be sown outdoors towards the end of May.

BAY

The proper name of this subject is *Laurus nobilis*, an evergreen shrub which should be grown in well-drained soil. It can be kept shapely by trimming each spring. The leaves, valuable for so many culinary purposes, are aromatic when crushed.

CARAWAY

This is a perennial which succeeds in good light soil. Sown in August really good plants should be available the following year. The seeds are very useful for flavouring cakes.

CHERVIL

This annual grows about a foot high having finely cut leaves and umbels of white flowers. A good herb for using in salads and for flavouring soups. Since the seed loses its germinating power quickly, it should be sown as soon as ripe.

CORIANDER

This is an attractive hardy annual of which the seeds have been used for centuries. When fully ripe the flavour is aromatic and when stored, the fragrance becomes stronger. Leaves are occasionally used in salads.

CUMIN

This rarely grown annual herb has been used medicinally for centuries, and it was once valued for flavouring cheese. The fennel-like plants a foot high, have dull pink flowers.

DANDELION

Anyone who has been troubled with weeds in the garden is unlikely to be very enthusiastic about growing dandelions. The young leaves are excellent in salads and may also be cooked. At one time dandelion tea was a remedy for liver troubles. When growing the plants the flower buds should be removed. The best way of cultivating dandelions is to sow seed in May and lift the roots early in November for forcing and blanching, since the green leaves are rather bitter.

DILL

A herb once commonly used for flavouring soups and pickles.

A decoction of the seed has long been used as a means of inducing sleep in children.

FENNEL

This perennial plant succeeds in any soil and it is easily raised from seed. Fennel sauce is said to make certain fish more digestible. *Finocchio dulce* is the Florence Fennel which usually produces a bulb at the base. These bulbs are stewed and served with melted butter.

HYSSOP

This is an old fashioned shrubby plant of which there are several species. The plants like light soil and full sun and should be kept clipped to keep them shapely. A few leaves cut up can help to improve a salad. It is not widely grown at the present time.

LAVENDER

Valued for their fragrance, their long period of flowering and their mid-grey foliage. These plants thrive in light well-drained soil. Lavender is one of the essentials in pot pourri. Reliable varieties include Twickel Purple with long purple spikes and Munstead Dwarf growing no more than 2ft.

LOVAGE

This perennial plant is notable for its handsome shiny foliage. The whole plant is aromatic the scent being suggestive of both celery and parsley. Useful for stews, soups and salads.

MARJORAM

There are several species the leaves of which impart a unique flavour to soups, whilst they are valued for bouquet garni.

MINT

This herb has many uses not the least being the value of the leaves for flavouring jellies and cordials. There are various kinds in cultivation including peppermint and spearmint and one often known as apple mint. It is spearmint that is most used for mint-sauce and this is one of the best for general cultivation, although it is susceptible to mint rust. To obtain fresh leaves throughout

I

the winter mint is sometimes forced in boxes or pots from November to May. In the garden, mint prefers a damp situation and need not be in full sunshine, although continuous shade leads to leggy growth.

PARSLEY

This is an ancient herb with health-giving qualities. It grows easily and is therefore valuable throughout the year. Hamburg Parsley is a distinct herb much used for winter salads, for the roots, similar to those of carrots, can be eaten raw, whilst the tops are used in the same way as parsley for flavouring and garnishing.

PENNYROYAL

This old fashioned, but still valuable herb of the mentha family has good flavouring qualities and dries well.

PURSLANE

This ancient plant has thick fleshy leaves and coloured stems. Always useful in salads and for other culinary purposes although flowering should be prevented otherwise the leaves deteriorate quickly.

RAMPION

This is a hardy biennial of which both the leaves and root are used. The latter can be sliced and eaten raw or cooked. The leaves too, are useful in salads.

RUE

This herb has certain medicinal qualities and was once widely used as a remedy for indigestion, rue tea being the way in which the health benefited.

SAGE

This is too well known to need description and has many uses both as a decorative plant and for using in stuffings.

SAVORY

The annual or summer savory is raised from seed sown in

April and has a flavour like that of marjoram. The leaves, finely chopped, are often used with broad beans. They are valued too for flavouring stuffings. Winter savory keeps its colour well in the darkest days and the leaves are used in soups and for stuffings. An old remedy for bee stings was to rub the affected part with the leaves.

SKIRRET

This little-known plant was once widely grown in Britain. The edible part is the cluster of branching roots which can be boiled or grated. The flavour is something like that of carrots or parsley. Sow the seed in the spring in sandy soil and the roots will be ready from September onwards.

SORREL

This perennial herb is used in soups, stews and salads. At one time it was largely used instead of apple sauce with poultry.

SWEET CICELY OR MYRRH

This is an attractive plant reaching 5ft. high with fern-like leaves. Both leaves and roots are used in salads. The roots should be boiled.

TANSY

Once a plant grown in almost every cottage garden, it was formerly used in Tansy cakes for the Easter Festival. There is now less liking for the pungent flavourings our ancestors used. A very small portion of a leaf is sufficient for chopping up and using in mixed salads. Tansy plants need watching since they are inclined to be rather invasive.

TARRAGON

This herb flourishes in sandy soil. There are several forms and Tarragon vinegar is flavoured with the foliage before the plants flower in late July.

THYME

This is one of the most used herbs. In the garden it makes

a splendid edging plant and the small dark green leaves are used for stuffings and seasonings. The lemon scented thyme gives out a delightful lemon flavour when used for cooking purposes.

Whilst herbs may not be essential they do contain ingredients which are invaluable to health. They help to bring out the flavour of many dishes and properly used, they greatly improve salads.

DRYING HERBS

Herbs available in shops cannot be compared with those dried straight from the garden. Leaves should be gathered before the plants come into flower, for flavour is then at its best. Cut them in the morning after the dew has dried off and before the sun is at its hottest. Never dry herbs in full sun or in strong winds, for the essential oils are then easily lost.

After rinsing in cold water, shake thoroughly, and tie in small loose bunches so that they dry gradually. They can be laid out on a table or other flat area but this means turning them twice a day. In a wet season it is possible to dry herbs in a very cool oven or leaves can be kept in the kitchen near the stove.

When dry, they can be rubbed to powder and placed in jars or other firmly corked containers.

Thyme.

CHAPTER 21

THE FRUIT GARDEN

Apart from the convenience of being able to gather fruit from one's own garden when it is in prime condition for harvesting, the difference in flavour between fruit eaten shortly after being gathered and that which has been in a shop or store for many days or even weeks makes it more than worthwhile to plant a few fruit trees and bushes, even in a small garden.

Large growing areas are not necessary for apart from bushes and standards many subjects can be had as single or double cordons or as espalier or fan-trained specimens. These will grow flat against a wall or fence or can be used for dividing the garden into separate parts. Currants and gooseberries can be grown as fruit hedges so long as the correct pruning procedure is carried out.

Ground in good heart, well prepared and enriched with bulky manure or other humus forming material, should be regarded as desirable before planting is carried out. Attention should be paid to drainage since no bush or tree will produce good quality fruit if its roots are waterlogged. Dry roots must also be avoided.

In the case of apples, pears, plums and cherries, root stocks are important although most of us are likely to grow the bushes or standards as supplied by the nurseryman without being concerned about the stocks. As a guide to apple stocks, they include the following: M.9 a dwarf stock, used where space is limited and early bearing is important. A much used vigorous stock is M.2.; while MM.104 is very strong rooting. Other widely used apple stocks include M.26, M.7, and MM.106.

Most pears are grafted on to Quince A or C stock. For plums Mussel, Brompton, St Julien and Myrobalan are used. For cherries Mazzards or St Lucie are reliable. Soft fruits are almost always propagated from cuttings.

The regular pruning and shaping of all fruit trees and bushes is advisable but even when this has been done there is sometimes lack of fruit. This can be due to frost damage or cultural fault, but often it is a matter of incomplete or entire lack of pollination and fertilisation. Therefore, when buying fruit trees it is wise to select self-fertile varieties or those which will cross-pollinate.

Advice on this matter will be readily given by nurserymen.

Planting distance for fruit trees will depend on their shape, the following is a guide to the space required. Bushes 12-14ft.; single cordons, planted at an angle of 45°, the tip towards the north, 2-2½ft. Espaliers and Fan-trained 15-18ft. Standards and half standards 20-24ft. These distances may seem great but they allow for development over the years. Apples on stock M.9 could be planted closer since they do not grow so large. Soft fruit bushes can be spaced from 3ft. apart.

Varieties are largely a matter of personal choice, but taking into consideration flavour, cropping and good healthy growth, the following may be depended upon. The figures after the name indicates the months the fruit is at its best.

Apples, dessert: Cox's Orange Pippin 11-1; Egremont Russet 9-10; Ellisons Orange 9, 10; James Grieve 9, 10; Laxton's Fortune 9-10; Laxton's Superb 12-2; Worcester Pearmain 7-9; *Apples, culinary*; Bramley Seedling 11-4; Arthur Turner 9-10; Lord Derby 11-1; Lanes Prince Albert 1-3; Newton Wonder 1-4. Charles Ross 9-11, is a first-class dual-purpose variety.

Nectarines: Early River and Elruge crop well in a sheltered place, as do Peaches Duke of York, Hale's Early and Peregrine.

Cherries: While the culinary variety Morello is self-fertile, all others need a pollinator if they are to crop well. Varieties include Early Rivers, Governor Wood and Napoleon Bigarreau.

Pears: William's Bon Chretien, ripens in August and September, while Beurre Hardy, Conference, Doyenne du Comice, Louise Bonne of Jersey and Fertility will be ready from October onwards. Winter Nelis, if stored well, remain in good condition from December to February. Less easy to obtain is Jarganelle with tender, melting flesh and Glou Morceau having firm flesh of good flavour. As in apples we require crisp and crunchable fruit, in pears, we look for soft texture, leading to silent consumption.

Plums: Victoria is still the most widely grown dessert variety. A heavy cropper, the oval bright red, fine flavoured fruit matures in September. Coe's Golden Drop, Cambridge Gage and Early Transparent Gage are also good. Dennistons Gage is greenish-yellow and Early Rivers a round black fruit ripening in August, and fine for dessert and bottling. Merryweather is a smallish plum with the true damson flavour. Well-drained soil which retains moisture in spring or summer is needed, especially in the case of trees trained against a wall. Soft fruits are notable for their quick returns. They come into bearing the second season after planting, and continue to yield for many years.

Currants: These are always in demand. Black currants are the most popular since they have more uses. They will grow satisfactorily on most soils that permit free rooting and where there is an adequate supply of moisture during the summer months. The addition of well rotted manure or other bulky feeding material will supply the nitrogen needs for young growth. Allow 4 to 5ft. between the bushes. Regular pruning in September consists of removing the old wood to make way for the young, lighter coloured-stems. Baldwin, Blacksmith and Seabrooks are reliable varieties. Red Currants favour rather lighter soils which do not lack potash. They will usually thrive even when planted under top fruit such as standard apples and pears. Pruning consists of cutting back the laterals right to their base. Summer pruning can consist of shortening the laterals which will encourage formation of fruit buds. White currants can be grown in a similar way.

Gooseberries are well worth cultivating and one may reckon that the bushes have a profitable life of twelve to fifteen years. For early crops, Whitesmith is good; Careless green, is grand for bottling; Leveller and Golden Drop are two good yellow dessert varieties; Whinhams Industry is red and rather hairy. Well-manured soil not lacking in potash suits this crop. When pruning, spur the laterals to within two buds of the base and shorten leading shoots.

Loganberries and the cultivated blackberries are useful for growing against walls and fences and so long as the old canes are cut out annually, there is no need for them to become a tangled mass.

Raspberries succeed best in deep, cool soil not lacking in moisture in summer, although drainage should be good. In the absence of farmyard manure, ' ripe ' compost and hop manure can be dug in. Plant the canes 15 to 18in. apart with 5 or 6ft. between rows. Old canes should be removed as soon as the fruit has been gathered. Lloyd George is still the most widely grown variety but there are other good sorts such as Malling Jewel, Norfolk Giant, and September, the latter being a fine late variety. A recent introduction is Zeva, a thornless variety, the large good flavoured berries being produced from July to November. Glen Clova is another fairly new variety, fruiting over a long period and most useful for dessert, jam, bottling and freezing.

Strawberries are invaluable. They prefer a good enriched

medium loam plentifully supplied with humus matter so that the roots do not dry out at any time. Select an open sunny but not an exposed or low lying position, and plant firmly, allowing a spacing of 15 to 18in. apart with 2 to 2½ft. between rows. September or early October is the best planting time. One-year bedded plants, or pot-grown specimens planted in the autumn, will normally produce a good crop the following year. Of the many varieties in cultivation Royal Sovereign remains popular, followed by Cambridge Favourite, Cambridge Vigour and Grandee which ripens from mid-June onwards. The giant fruit weighs 2 to 3oz. and is good-flavoured. The Remontants are continuous fruiting varieties, and include St Claude and Sans Rivale. The Alpine varieties, particularly Baron Solemacher, a non-runeing sort, are useful for cropping from August onwards. Although the berries are smaller than those of the more usual varieties, the flavour is excellent. Red and white alpine strawberries are also worth growing, the fruit, although small, being of a rich buttery flavour.

Less common fruits which can be cultivated without undue trouble and which the gardener will find most rewarding include *figs,* which given a warm position, can be grown against a wall. A gravelly porous loam over a chalky subsoil is suitable. Drainage should be good although plenty of water should be available during the growing season. Where the soil is very deep, the practice of placing a slate or large stone 12in. or so under the tree when planting is recommended. This prevents the formation of a tap root and lots of foliage to the exclusion of fruit. Figs can also be grown in pots outdoors, being taken into the greenhouse when severe weather threatens.

Grape vines are now being grown outdoors in many parts of the country. They flourish in a wide range of soils. Waterlogging and sour root conditions must be avoided. The end of October is a good planting time spacing the vines 4 to 4½ft. apart. Regular annual pruning is necessary. Many named varieties are available including: Chasselas Rose, pinkish ornamental berries and Noir Hatif de Marseilles, large clusters of black fruit. Brandt and Concord are excellent for wine purposes.

Mespilus germanica is the Medlar, which with Quince, has comparatively few edible uses but bush or standard trees of both are interesting and ornamental in any garden.

The mulberry (*Morus*) is both decorative and fruiting, the trees being of attractive appearance at all times. The sweet-flavoured fruit assumes a dark crimson colour from August onwards.

There is no doubt that home-grown fruit is a pleasure to cultivate and a joy to eat. As Edward Buyard the fruit grower and connoisseur of some generations ago, once wrote ' the apple not only keeps the doctor from our doors but ourselves from the dentists '. The eating of more fresh fruit would undoubtedly contribute much more to good health than the ready prepared foods from tins so popular at the present time.

CHAPTER 22

GREENHOUSE GARDENING

THE POSSESSION of a greenhouse greatly increases the enjoyment of a garden. Where the area is large, a glasshouse usually becomes a necessity for raising new stock and for providing protection for bedding-plants which cannot stand the winter outdoors. In addition, a well-furnished greenhouse will, especially where some heat is available, be a source of pleasure in providing a cheerful display throughout the year and in furnishing cut flowers and pot plants for living-room decoration. One or two garden frames, a propagator, and a potting shed are other luxuries which will provide great pleasure and reward.

There are many types of greenhouses on the market, the three standard types being the span or ridge, the three-quarter span, and the lean-to. Recently however other shapes have made their appearance notably the round greenhouse. It is also possible to use a glazed porch as a greenhouse provided it is made as draught-free as possible.

More simply, the so-called Dutch lights which are large sheets of glass about 65in. by 48in. held in a wooden frame, can be used for many purposes. They are particularly useful for covering crops grown in the soil rather than in pots. This includes crops such as tomatoes, carnations, and chrysanthemums. It is also possible to erect staging for the use of pot plants. Although cheaper being all glass, they need far more heat.

The traditional style of greenhouse, with low walls of brick, concrete or wood, has many advantages. It preserves heat in winter and is not subject to the same fluctuations in temperature as an all-glass structure.

Metal houses are now widely used, but wood is still depended upon by the majority of gardeners. The type of wood to be used will influence cost and may be summed up as follows:

Very durable –   teak, western red cedar, oak.
Durable   –   long leaf pitch pine.
Not durable   –   Norway spruce or 'white wood'.

The life of woodwork can be greatly prolonged by treating it with a preservative. Linseed oil used on teak and red cedar, will produce a mature appearance as well as safeguard against premature rotting. White lead paint should be used since this reflects light. Hinges must not be neglected.

Steel and aluminium alloy are much used, the latter being easier to shape. Concrete houses which are reinforced with iron rods are strong and durable, but much less elegant looking.

Before taking delivery, try to inspect a model of the house you intend to buy, for some of the mass-produced 'lines' are not always of as good quality as one would wish. Make sure doors and ventilators fit properly. Take note too, of the placing of the ventilators which in small greenhouses should be placed along the apex ridge. Make sure the foundations are right with a proper getaway for water from the greenhouse surrounds.

Prominence has been given to the use of glass substitutes. Stringent tests have shown that there is nothing to compete with glass in the long run, although polythene and other forms of plastic can be used on certain occasions. Glass is easier to clean, it does not scratch and the full quality of light is transmitted.

Plastic is of value as an inner lining for greenhouses especially those without heat, preventing the temperature from falling very low at night. For this purpose it must be fitted properly to prevent condensation-drips falling on plants. It is also possible to use plastic for shading and to give protection from wind, rain and draughts.

The heating of greenhouses can be done in several ways and although coal and coke boilers are still efficient they make more work by having to be stoked during the winter. Paraffin heaters are much cheaper to install although perhaps, not much cheaper to run in structures of any size. They need daily attention and the volume of heat cannot be controlled to counteract temperature changes outside. If using an oil stove always choose one with a blue flame.

Electricity is perhaps the most expensive, but certainly the least troublesome form of heating, since there is no stoking or trimming to be done. It is important to have the equipment installed by a qualified electrician who will be able to connect the supply to the mains. Once electricity is available many types of greenhouse equipment, including thermostats and fans, can be used.

Tubular heating is simple to install although fans are easier to move and they blow warm air, which seems agreeable to plants, through the house. In addition, water-filled heaters provide humidity as well as heat thus creating good conditions for many plants. Electric thermostatic control provides unvarying temperatures which cannot be achieved by other forms of heating.

Electricity is useful for soil warming and can be done by burying warming cables in the frame or hot bed. Cover them with a good 6in. layer of soil. The installation of such cables needs to be done by a knowledgeable person so that accidents do not occur.

The old fashioned method of heating greenhouses by large hot water pipes from outside boilers fired by various means is still very efficient. It is not one that the amateur gardener is likely to choose from choice or convenience, for their use certainly means that they have to be stoked at night. Many people who originally had this type of heater have now changed to oil or electricity which are both easier to manage and probably cheaper to run.

The siting of any greenhouse is important, and will have some influence on the amount of artificial heat required. Full sun exposure is advisable so there are no shadows from trees or buildings. Avoid positions exposed to north or east winds. Houses are usually placed in a north-south position, although east to west alignment improves the transmission of light.

The house fitments need careful selection and proper staging is essential. Slatted staging while useful is not ideal, since it is liable to be draughty. It is better to use fibre glass or galvanised iron, and to cover this with small pebbles or weathered ashes to a depth of 2in. If this is kept moist it will greatly reduce the work of watering and lead to better growth.

A good thermometer is required, also a syringe, fine rosed watering can, one or two sieves, a trowel and a potting stick. Necessary adjuncts to the greenhouse are a good light potting shed and one or two frames. A propagator or miniature greenhouse, a foot square, will be useful for raising difficult plants.

Growing plants in a greenhouse is really cultivating them under artificial conditions. Apart from the soil in which they are put to grow there are some basic needs that plants have if they are to succeed. Tidiness and cleanliness are important so the greenhouse should be kept clean and not used as a junk shed. Protection must be given from natural enemies such as insects, pests, fungus diseases and virus. Plants need feeding since they cannot always obtain all the nourishment they need from the greenhouse soil, or soil in pots. All plants grown in the greenhouse need light, although some less than others.

There are various means of providing shade from strong

summer sunshine, some gardeners prefer to paint the glass with Summer Cloud or whiting, whilst others depend on sun blinds made from various materials.

Ventilation goes hand in hand with heat control and humidity, and it is only experience which enables one to have the right judgment in this connection. Plants vary in their atmospheric needs, but generally it is best to avoid very dry atmospheres as well as those which are heavy and stuffy. Humidity is largely influenced by watering methods, much less water being needed during colder weather. Over-watering is always likely to cause disorders.

Many plants need feeding, but do not apply fertilisers while they are dormant or when the soil is dry or the temperature very low. It is safest to depend on organic fertilisers rather than those which are over-rich in nitrogen or quick-acting, since these lead to rapid growth, which is much more liable to be susceptible to disease and pest attacks. The feeding of plants needs to be done with care and it is unwise to give additional feeding material after potting on or potting off. For plants in normal growth, the widely advertised liquid fertilisers can be relied upon. These include Liquinure and Maxicrop, while Clay's Fertiliser is a reliable powder feed. Organic manures and fertilisers lead to the build up of healthy growth.

There are many modern aids to greenhouse management. These include methods of easily controlling heating and ventilation. Then there is the air circulator which by its continuous gentle movement of the air, reduces condensation and leads to better plant health. Rollshades which guard plants against scorching sun or excessive heat can be pulled down or let up quickly and easily. In addition, if fitted to both sides of the house they help to retain heat on cold winter nights.

The so-called Tricklematic waterer is a simple but ingenious system for greenhouse borders, trays, benches and pot plants that require a supply of water to be released at set periods. Gravel trays for pots on greenhouse staging hold moisture and provide humidity around the plants to keep them healthy.

The Humex Moisture Metre lets you know when pot plants require moisture; the long probe is inserted into the soil and the dial instantly registers wet, moist or dry.

There are several easy to use propagators which serve as miniature heated greenhouses to be used inside the ordinary greenhouse where a higher temperature is needed and where it would be uneconomical to raise the temperature of the whole house.

With at least some of these fitments, greenhouse gardening is much easier and the results more sure than they could have been a few years ago.

THERMOMETERS

Although it is possible to grow a wide range of plants successfully in the greenhouse without the help of instruments the possession of a thermometer and a hygrometer does make it easier to keep the air temperature and air moisture under control.

Very few plants like or will tolerate wide temperature fluctuations. Both leaves and flowers wilt, plants become a poor colour, may fail to grow at all, and sometimes decay. The use of a good thermometer makes it possible to keep a check on warmth, for excessively high temperatures can be just as harmful as low ones.

One of the best thermometers to use is the Maximum and Minimum type which records the highest and lowest temperatures obtained. On this type, the tiny indicators are pushed up by the mercury but remain in position when the temperature falls. In really large houses, several of these thermometers can be placed in different positions and heights.

Soil thermometers are also useful especially on soil warming benches and in heated frames as well as when soil sterilising. They are also helpful for checking seed-sowing composts since some seeds will not germinate until the soil is sufficiently warm. Another use is for testing the warmth in a mushroom bed or a compost heap.

Apart from the well-known mercury and glass thermometers which are probably the best types, there are some dial instruments which operate by the expansion and contraction of a special metal coil. Whatever thermometer you buy, get the best you can afford, since in a continual moist greenhouse atmosphere, the scales may deteriorate in time.

HYGROMETERS

Atmospheric conditions play an important part in the general development of plants, just as much as they do in the lives of human beings. All plants need a certain amount of atmospheric moisture, although some deteriorate if the air becomes too heavily charged with moisture.

The experienced greenhouse gardener can sometimes tell when

his plants are suffering because of wrong air conditions. This, however, is usually a matter of guessing, and it is easy to make mistakes which can have adverse effects and make all the difference between success and failure. It is thus advisable to rely on instruments which give the answers accurately.

The hygrometer is an instrument by which the relative humidity of the atmosphere can be registered and recorded accurately on a dial. Although these instruments have been in use for some time, they have been regarded by amateur gardeners as being complicated and very few indoor gardeners have taken advantage of them.

The majority of plants in active growth will thrive in a humidity of from 60 to 80 per cent. The idea of checking the atmospheric moisture content of the greenhouse or living-room should not be regarded as a difficult problem. By using a good hygrometer it is a simple matter to ensure that conditions are right.

Air, of course, does sometimes enter the greenhouse in a saturated condition during damp, close weather, but once it becomes warmed, some of the moisture is extracted, since it is used by the floor, staging, the soil and the plants themselves. On the other hand when moist air is cooled off, it rids itself of the excess. This can often be seen on cool surfaces. This means that a relatively dry, warm atmosphere in the greenhouse at nightfall, may move toward saturation point as the temperature falls and when this happens the moisture droplets are deposited in various places.

It is because some plants need more atmospheric moisture at certain times of the year than others, that a hygrometer is such a useful adjunct. We have only to think of the conditions required by cacti, and say melons, to realise how different are the atmospheric conditions needed if success with these plants is to be achieved.

FROST WARNING DEVICES

What may be considered a luxury instrument is a frost warning device. This is of particular use in protecting fruit trees when the blossoms are opening in the spring. The important feature in this device is what is known as a sensing element which must be of material not subject to changes in weather conditions. Mercury, which has stood the test of centuries as an accurate and stable means of temperature measure is best suited to the purpose.

Such devices are hermetically sealed and not, therefore, subject to atmospheric influence resulting in corrosion, contamination or erosion. It is also essential to exclude from the circuitry, any contacting mechanism open to the atmosphere and liable to failure. All contacts used must, therefore, have Mercury Switches which are hermetically sealed. Soldered joints, correctly varnished, must be used for all exposed connections.

Regarding the Aural Warning device, this should, for preference, be an alternating current system which does not rely upon mechanical contact for its operation. The system is fed by electricity, and mounted on the control panel are two signals, one red and one green. When the temperature is higher than the danger point a green light indicates that all is in order, when it falls below the set point the red signal will show and at the same time sound the alarm.

CHAPTER 23

TERRARIUMS AND BOTTLE GARDENS

THE RATHER formidable sounding word terrarium, is often used as an analogy to describe a closed glass jar containing soil for plants, instead of one holding water for fish which we refer to as an aquarium.

Over a hundred and twenty-five years ago a London doctor, Nathaniel Ward, discovered that plants would live for years in a lidded glass jar without water or change of air and, apparently regardless of their outside environment. Now many types of terrarium are in use and can be made without difficulty. Plants in glass cases are protected from dust, draughts and harmful gases while changes of outside temperature are felt very gradually. Moisture evaporated by the soil and transpired by the leaves condenses on the glass and runs back into the soil, so there is no loss of water and there is always the right humidity.

The one drawback, however, is that condensation often prevents one from seeing the plants inside. It is therefore better to abandon the tightly closed case and allow some ventilation. This means that water will be needed, perhaps once every six months.

All manner of glass containers can be used such as large sweet jars, goldfish bowls, wine bottles and carboys. The clear types are better than those made of green glass. It is essential with carboys and all other glass containers to wash them thoroughly inside and out. Allow them to dry completely to prevent the soil sticking to the glass.

Into the bottom of the glass container put an inch or so of gravel, small pieces of broken flower pots, and similar rough material. Over this spread about 3in. of prepared soil mixture such as John Innes Compost No. 2, with a little lump charcoal added. See that these materials are just moist, not wet.

An easy way of getting the soil into the bottle is to pour it in through a strong paper funnel. A number of long-handled tools will be needed. Some can be bought, others can easily be made. Essentials include a spatula for digging little holes in the compost, a blunt-ended stick for dibbling, a pronged 'scratcher' for covering roots, a tamper for firming, and a pair of tweezers for inserting the plants.

K

It is possible to buy suitable tools of this kind, but most can easily be made. Tweezers or tongs can be made out of split bamboo canes. A teaspoon or an eggspoon wired to a metal rod can be used as a planting tool. A little block of wood fastened to a cane will act as a tamper, while a spatula will be useful for making little holes when new plants are being introduced.

Plant with restraint for a crowded appearance must be avoided. If you break off any leaves hook them out with a piece of bent wire. Keep soil off the foliage. Once planting is complete apply a fine mist spray of water to clean and freshen the leaves and to moisten the soil.

Although it is not essential to stopper the bottle garden, remember that the plants will grow larger if they are not entirely enclosed. This means a loss of water by evaporation, and occasional light watering will be necessary. Too much watering leads to the rotting of the roots and disease of the leaves.

What to plant needs careful consideration; a wrong choice could mean the whole bottle becoming choked with growth in a few months. Avoid *tradescantias* and *chlorophytum* and depend on small growing subjects. Suitable plants include small ferns, *peperomias*, fibrous begonias and *cryptanthus*. Use *neathe* or *cordyline* for centre positions and *saintpaulias* are suitable so long as you remove dying or mildewed leaves and flowers as soon as seen.

CHAPTER 24

THE OPEN-AIR SWIMMING-POOL

A SWIMMING pool can be a strong focal point in any garden. Obviously the space available must be sufficient to allow plenty of room for other garden features. There is no need for the pool to be square or oblong. In fact, it is better that it should be of a somewhat irregular shape so that it fits in with the surroundings and although a dominant feature, that it does not blot out the attractiveness of the flower border or rock garden.

It can be framed by a lawn but paved surrounds are probably better since there will then be no unsightly worn turf. The paving can be directed to a sun room or terrace.

The siting of the pool needs considerable thought so that it is placed to best advantage and this includes imagining what the pool and its surroundings will look like in a few years' time. It is not simply a question of digging a large hole and lining it, for apart from actual swimming in the pool, the surrounds should be made suitable for leisure activities. More time is spent around the water, rather than in it as a general rule. Many people who may not wish to bathe, like to sit or lie within sight of a pool of which the surrounds should be made as attractive as possible.

If it is possible to build a dry wall around the pool, this will be an added attraction, since it will not only give shelter from winds but make it possible to grow plants in the wall interstices. Suitable plants include: aubrietia in separate colours, *Alyssum saxatile*, armeria, *Campanula muralis*, helianthemums, sedums and *saxifrages*. Wall boxes of plants can also be used.

While the siting of the pool and its surrounds, including the terrace, sun room, and the placing of shrubs and trees, will depend on the size and shape of the garden, certainly a seat or two, judiciously placed, perhaps recessed into a wall or group of shrubs, will break the horizon and always be attractive. Display borders of colourful plants; pots, tubs and similar containers of plants placed at vantage points, and a few trees for windbreaks will all improve the site.

Do not plant trees or shrubs too near the water for, otherwise, leaves blowing or falling into the pool will need to be cleaned out as they will otherwise foul the water. Fallen leaves are also liable to lead to bathers slipping on the surrounds.

In recent years the demand for liner pools has greatly increased. These offer the advantages of the conventional concrete pool but are mostly constructed from factory-made components which can be quickly assembled on the site a reasonably low cost.

It is essential to make the best possible pool and one which is designed to withstand all stresses and strains likely to arise. There are models available in which all the structural components are resistant to corrosion and in which the virtually indestructible glass reinforced fibre is used. This means that with a properly made pool there is no risk of wall movement or collapse when the pool is emptied.

In the best examples, the pool floor is finished with a cement and sand screed for added strength, plus a special composition to prevent the surface from cracking before it is covered with a heavy gauge vinyl liner. If a main drain is fitted it improves water circulation as well as being invaluable should it ever be decided to empty the pool.

In the ' Ambassador ' pools, special care is taken to use only the best tested materials which will withstand years of hard wear. Ambassador pools also include many exclusive extras such as the Cyclolac skimmer which takes the water from the surface of the pool and passes it through a floating peripheral weir and strainer basket, which traps floating debris from the surface.

Underwater lighting greatly enhances the appearance of a pool after dark and enables swimming to continue into the late evening. The light can be placed in any position but preferably at the deep end. In fact, several can be installed at vantage points. Make sure each underwater light is operated from a 12 volt transformer. It is strongly recommended that all light installations are carried out by a qualified electrical engineer.

There are available a number of accessories the use of which will add to the enjoyment of the possession of a swimming-pool. These include a stainless steel three-step ' ladder ' for use as steps into the pool, an upright floating thermometer calibrated in fahrenheit and centigrade, a pool brush for cleaning floor and walls and a special test kit supplied with full instructions for testing the condition of the pool water and the amount of chlorine present.

Swimming-pools can be heated by oil, gas, or electricity and details of running costs can be worked out by contacting the local offices of these heating services.

CHAPTER 25

THE DELIGHTS OF A SAUNA

FOR MORE than a thousand years the people of Finland have been enjoying the quite unique delights of sauna bathing. Now you too can change your way of life and introduce your family to one of the most sensational ways there is of keeping fit. The pace and strain of modern living leaves its mark on us all. We all make big demands on our systems: the pressure of business, the tension of driving, the demands of social obligations, the strain of bringing up children, even the concentration of studying.

A sauna bath can be described as an enclosed timber cubicle with a double skin which contains insulating material. An electric stove is located inside with its controls and thermostat fitted on the outer wall. The stove creates either moist or dry heat which is circulated partly by convection and partly by the ventilation system of the room. Inside there is a duckboard floor and slatted benches on which bathers can sit or lie. Other standard fitments include a double-glazed window, lights and, of course, the special sauna rocks which create steam when water is poured over them. Saunas are produced in various sizes ranging from about four feet square for the small house up to more than 10ft. by 7ft. for sporting clubs, etc.

Regular bathing in your sauna will iron out the stresses of modern life and relieve tense muscles. It relaxes yet refreshes you at the same time. It aso cleans out the pores of your skin in a way that no conventional washing or showering can ever do. You will emerge from your sauna feeling really invigorated. After a short rest, you will feel in a better frame of body and mind than even a good night's relaxing sleep could possibly induce. There is nothing quite like it.

Medically, sauna bathing has the approval of doctors for all but sufferers of a few very special ailments. It gives the body total change. Perspiration combined with the heat itself is good exercise for the skin, and – ladies – it contributes to the complexion too. Sauna bathing is normally accompanied by a drop in blood pressure of between ten and fifteen per cent. This is quickly restored by the stimulation of a cold shower or bath and by a period of relaxation.

As a direct slimming aid, sauna bathing has only limited value, for although perspiration will induce a weight loss of up to six pounds, most of this will be replaced by the normal intake of liquid. Nevertheless, sauna is a useful prelude to many of the accepted slimming therapies. Your sauna bath will make a direct contribution to the good health and happiness of the whole family.

If you have yet to experience the delights of sauna bathing, let's assume you've just installed a new sauna in your home and you want to devote an hour or so to replacing what the demands of the day have taken from you. First, switch on the heater of your sauna to a pre-set temperature (probably between 200° and 250° F) and give it ten minutes or so to warm up. Meanwhile use this time to take a swift shower or bath.

Enter the sauna and sit or recline on one of the benches. You will immediately be engulfed in the hot, dry heat of the stove which will soon generate perspiration. Sit back and let the sauna feeling get to work on your whole body. To create steam, pour a little water from the traditional wooden pail over the rocks in the stove. After fifteen or twenty minutes, if you want to follow the true Finnish practice, it's time for a cool shower or bath.

The process can be repeated as often as you like, although you will obviously want to be a little cautious at first while you experiment and find the temperature which suits you best. An ideal temperature for beginners is about 175° F. The whole family can join in this healthy and enjoyable pastime.

After sauna, the sudden cold shock of the shower increases the adrenalin secretion and the heart action speeds up, the senses are sharpened, reaction speed increases and capillaries carry the blood heated by the internal organs to the surface for cooling which steps up the surface circulation again. With so much extra work for the body to do there is a complete mental and physical relaxation.

Complete relaxation alone can bring untold benefits to the recipient. It is estimated that sixty per cent of our ailments, including those conditions usually associated with rheumatism and arthritis, stem from nervous tension. Muscular aches and pains can be eased by the caressing heat, and tensions unwound by the luxurious feeling within the body after the sauna.

Where in the home is the best place to install your new sauna? Obviously, this must be decided before you can select the model and layout of your choice, so take a quick look around your house to find the ideal position. If you live in an older property, the bathroom or landing may well provide space for a sauna. If so, all the better, because it will be handily placed close to the bath or shower. In the newer home it is unlikely that either of these places will be large enough, but there are many other possibilities. The first to spring to mind is obviously the spare bedroom or boxroom. Utility and laundry rooms can make an ideal home for a sauna, as can the attic if access is easy. Remember, too, that your sauna installation is not a permanent fixture, it can always be moved at some future date.

Large garages, particularly those with a connecting door·to the house, have been very successfully partitioned to create a sauna room. Sunrooms and home extensions are also ideal. There are even odd corners within the house itself which offer possibilities. How much space for example is there under your stairs? Maybe there's an alcove within a room which could be curtained off. Perhaps you could dispense with a cloakroom downstairs; remember that you can still hang coats in there when the sauna is not in use. Or can you convert the basement?

Don't forget that when you have found the ideal spot for your sauna you are not necessarily abandoning the use of the space for other purposes. Indeed, with a little judgment, you can make use of your sauna room for many purposes when you are not actually enjoying a refreshing bath. For example, it could be used for drying clothes particularly on a wet winter's day. With the heater safely unplugged, you can turn the sauna room over to the chilren as a ' den '. If necessary, you can even convert it into an overnight guest-room.

When you have chosen the ideal place for your sauna, for which you will need a clear height of 6ft. 10in. you can select the model which is best suited to the available space and to the size of your family. Don't forget that the capacity of your sauna will be governed by whether you wish to lie or sit inside it. Good ventilation is important, not only to enable you to enjoy a sauna bath at its traditional best but also to ensure that the bath itself remains fresh and clean.

CHAPTER 26

BARBECUING FOR YOU

PARTICULARLY IN summer when many meals can be eaten out of doors there is an added interest in having a barbecue party. This can be done without great expense or inconvenience but there are several important points to consider before you set up the barbecue. It can, with proper arrangement, become an attractive feature as well as a practical one and can be chosen in the same way as one selects garden furniture.

There are now literally scores of designs in different sizes and it is really worth while taking some trouble to choose a barbecue to scale with your garden. Siting is also important and a position as sheltered as possible, preferably one protected by a wall, fence, or bushes, which form a satisfactory windbreak. This too, will help to govern the direction of any smoke.

Suitable paving underneath and around will be an advantage particularly since lawn and other grass areas can become slippery in damp weather, and look unsightly when they become worn and patchy. Another point to consider is to site the barbecue where there are no steps or difficult places to manoeuvre.

Adequate lighting is also important. To go with many of the modern barbecues, outdoor lighting equipment is available much of which is very ornamental, although the old fashioned hurricane lamps hung from hooks fixed nearby, add a romantic touch to the occasion.

With any good barbecue there are supplied tongs, pokers and forks. It is best to choose those with long wooden handles since metal becomes hot. Choice of fuel will depend on the type of barbecue being used, although charcoal or special charcoal briquettes are excellent since they burn longer without stoking. Briquettes unless specially treated, require several minutes of intense heat to become ignited. They absorb moisture regularly and in very humid weather may become hard to kindle and slow to glow. There are also gas fired and electric models although young people in particular find these less fun than using charcoal.

The Structo gas-fired grills are easy to run and have come through many tests for performance. Most of this type have a round-shaped grill which has proved ideal for their superior cooking ability through a concentration of heat radiation; being round they do not lose heat in the corners. Gas barbecues can be used instantly. With each gas grill six pounds of natural lava rock is included. This converts the gas flame to radiant heat for finest barbecue cooking.

There are two types of covered barbecue outfits. The Kettle grill has a cover that rests on the bowl to make an air-tight seal around the cooking space within. This means it will not only contain the fire's heat but reflect this heat back from all sides to the cooking food. The cover can be lifted off or so hinged to serve as a windbreak. Air vents in the cover and bowl bottom, control draughts.

The fire bowl is on a removable grate, the grill or grid being above this at the top of the bowl. The best models have a built-in thermometer in the cover as an indication of inside heat. An internal baffle acts as a distributor for both draughts and heating material. With some models a useful spit attachment is provided.

The Wagon grill is rectangular, having a built-on hood with hinged fold-back front door. This fully encloses the space above the cooking grill which, however, does not become air-tight. Draught controls are in the hood and in some cases there is also a warming shelf at the top of the hood.

The hood is equipped with a spit and motor for rotisserie cooking. Below the grill is an adjustable-height grate and below this, a removable ash pan which when removed, leaves the bottom open. The most convenient Wagon models are those with a built-in thermometer, a clear vision glass panel in the hood cover, a charcoal feeder door and a cutting board. Both the Kettle and Wagon grills give the option of open or covered grilling with opportunity for rotisserie cooking.

Round bowl grills or braziers are available in many styles. The steel bowl holds both charcoal and ashes as well as supporting the wire grill used for cooking. The types with a windbreak of some kind and with legs, are the most desirable. Some models have legs with wheels for easy transport; others have folding legs which makes carrying and storage simple.

CAMPER'S OUTFIT

The Camper's barbecue must be lightweight and easy to carry in a single package with no special parts that could be left behind. There are a number of models of this type on the market with such features as a windbreak, an adjustable-height grill, legs and a spit.

A number of specialised outfits can also be obtained so that the fun of barbecuing need not be limited to fair weather days or evenings. Models are available designed so that the barbecue fire can be used safely indoors while still producing all the flavour of outdoor cooking.

IN THE HOUSE

The table grill has an air-vented grate and an adjustable-height grill; some types have legs. The fireplace grill, popular in the United States, can be used where a chimney will carry off smoke. Most of these have a swing out grill so that there is no need to bend head and shoulders into the fireplace when tending the food.

COOKING METHOD

Grilling is done with the firebed located directly beneath the food to be cooked, which is laid on the grill. This is suitable for meats which have to be cooked fast. Direct heat at close range will keep in juices and create an exterior crust. The distance between grill and fuel will govern how quickly and deeply the ' crust ' forms.

By reflected heat application, the heat is indirectly applied to the sides rather than the bottom of the meat. Where there is a cover or hood, the heat is also reflected back. In a Kettle Grill heat reflection is so concentrated that it is applied uniformly all round. This type of heating is suitable for cooking large cuts of meat, whole chickens, fish and ' baked ' meat pies. Little or no turning is required and flavour is retained by this method.

Smoke Cooking at first, might not seem very desirable but some people do like a smoked flavour. A Kettle grill or Wagon grill does not produce this type of flavour unless smoke is artificially created. This is done by sprinkling selected, dampened wood chips on the coals. It is sometimes possible to buy packets of suitable chips and apple wood and hickory are said to be the best for this purpose. The smoke is held inside the grill by adjusting the air vents, the dampened wood providing the smoke which imparts the special flavour.

Recipes with various aids showing how to increase efficiency in use are usually distributed with all grills.

INDEX